The Spirit Of Python Unveiled

In

OPERATION PYTHON DETHRONING THE FALSE PROPHET

by Paula Cross

© Copyright 2012 - Paula Cross

All right reserved. This book is protected by the copyright laws of the United States of America. This book may not be copied or reprinted. Please inquire if bulk purchases are necessary; rates will be adjusted for volume orders.

Scripture quotations marked NIV are taken from THE HOLY BIBLE, NEW INTERNATIONAL VERSION, Copyright ©1984, 2005, 2010 by International Bible Society. Used by permission of Zondervan. All Rights Reserved. KING JAMES VERSION quotations are marked with KJV and are public domain. Scripture quotations marked NLT are taken from The Holy Bible, New Living Translation, copyright © 1996, 2004, 2007. Used by permission of Tyndale House Publishers, Inc. Carol Stream, Illinois 60188. All Rights Reserved.

Cover: Photo by Tiberiu Sahlean; a contributing photographer of Dreamstime.com. Cover Layout Design by Paula Cross. Interior Photo by Kagenomai. Disclaimer: The usage of these images is not necessarily an endorsement of the photographers other artistic endeavors.

The passages quoted from Encyclopedia Britannica are kindly permitted "By courtesy of Encyclopedia Britannica, Inc., copyright 2012; used with permission."

Definitions quoted from the Merriam-Webster Dictionary are permitted "By permission. From Merriam-Webster's Collegiate® Dictionary, 11th Edition©2011 by Merriam-Webster, Incorporated (www.merriam-webster.com)" and is notated accordingly at the bottom of the page as per their request. Material quoted from the book Secret Teachings of all Ages: Wonders of Antiquity by Manly P. Hall; 1928 - [Copyright not renewed] are public domain. Excerpts quoted from pg 50-51 of *John G. Lake - His Life, His Sermons, His Boldness of Faith*; Published by KCP Kenneth Copeland Publications, Fort Worth Texas. ©1994 Kenneth Copeland Publications.

www.paulacross.com

ISBN-13: 978-1490588469
ISBN-10: 1490588469

Table of Contents

CHAPTER	PAGE
Introduction	1
01 – The Many Faces of Python	7
02 – Signs That Python Has A Grip	15
03 – The Beginning of A Dark Kingdom	29
04 – Understanding The Kingdoms	41
05 – The Rise of The False Prophet	51
06 – It's Just A Namesake	67
07 – Dancing With The Devil	85
08 – When You Seek Me With All Your Heart	101
09 – Confounded By Constriction	119
10 – Python & Our Finances	135
11 – Condemnation: One Slick Tool	151
12 – Praise, Power & Position	159
13 – Victory Nay Embraced	171
14 – Law VS Grace	183
15 – Withstanding The Resistance	195
16 – Forever Abiding	213
My Heart's Desire Evaluation	231

Introduction

It's no secret.... The devil is out to steal, kill, and destroy. But once we are redeemed and since we are children of a MIGHTY God, aren't we supposed to be victors over darkness? Why do dark clouds still follow some of us as though they can – and prevail? And why does God not rescue us from their power? How do curses dominate our lives even after we've 'broken them off'? Why do we keep going in the same cycles of defeat? Where is our God?

I've been perplexed over this for years. I'm a Christian. And my God is Master of the Universe! He is the ALMIGHTY! And His Word promises that I would have life and have it to the full. Yet, despite being a daughter of the Most High, the darkness is what has prevailed over my soul and the circumstances of my life. I couldn't understand how things could be this way... until now.

After giving my life to the Lord and spending more than twenty years consciously following Jesus Christ but suffering at the hands of darkness, I have discovered that I belonged to God but was *dominated* by the spirit of python.

The spirit of python, a powerful ruler of darkness, is being exposed like never before. In fact, this mighty ancient worker has accomplished too many victories to number yet is painstakingly nervous because of what the Holy Spirit is doing right this very moment! What He is doing for you... What He is doing for me. Glory be to our God. Eyes are being opened and the python is losing ground in lives of even those he's had the most deeply rooted generational grip upon.

The fact is the python spirit's origin is rooted in mythology. But kid you not, the profound faith in the ancient Greek's system of beliefs and false gods emanated from their culture is what gave this spirit a grand platform!

This book will establish just who the spirit of python really is and how it can be that our lives today are so adversely affected by this strong man of old even when and especially after giving our lives to the Lord. We will discuss how the introduction of python had its premise in idolatry and divination yet how a vast empire emerged which infiltrated the Church of God. It will be shown that the spirit of python is more than a singular principality but is an elaborate operation hell-bent on wiping out all that is spiritually true, right, and holy.

In 1996 I saw a vision of something coiled around my body and later God told me it was a python which was the first time I'd ever heard of such a thing. And it was the only time I was aware of the entity being at work in my life until 2009 when God revealed that I, like many in the church, had been one of the spirit of python's long term projects. The Holy Spirit revealed how it is that this spirit is actually an empire of dark forces out to stifle the church and ultimately, the POWER of GOD. Bottom line: squash, suffocate, hinder, delay, distract, oppress, destroy, or in the least, twist Paula all up in knots – and do the same to everyone else who has the potential to walk with Christ in power.

Many are teaching how to recognize and deal with the spirit of python. The problem is we don't know who he really is. The best way to explain it is to compare the dark kingdom to the military. In the military, the attacks and legwork are implemented by the lower ranks while the majors, colonels, and "**generals**" are the organizers and strategists who oversee and instruct the lower ranks. The dark kingdom's army is much the same which means all the attacks and strategies that are implemented are done by lower ranking minions. They are assigned to do x, y, and z. The troubles people experience are the x, y, and z's at the hands of these minions. But the minions are not the organizers nor are they the strategists. These minions are simply carrying out their assignments.

Now where do we suppose the spirit of python ranks in this vast army? It seems the perspective is that he is of lower rank because he is the one who comes in for the kill - to constrict and suffocate slowly through various strategies. He's the one throwing the grenades, so to speak. While this is correct, the problem is all we perceive is the immediate attackers and this is why most remain under the dominion of Python. The question is who is the one strategizing and giving the orders that these snakes are implementing? Another question is why does it matter where the top orders come from since it's obvious that Satan is the one behind it all?

It does matter. Let's look at another military analogy. If the military advances into a territory, they are attacking and doing damage but when they occupy, the regime then has control. The dark kingdom works the same. The low ranking minions are forever attacking and doing damage. But the situation is different and worse if the regime occupies and takes control of the territory.

What most people teach on concerning the spirit of python is how these low ranking snakes attack and do damage. Everyone experiences these attacks by default by being born on this earth. And it is important to understand all that has been taught, absolutely. The problem is nothing is being taught to those whose lives have been taken over, or "occupied" by the regime. For those who are occupied, their lives are dominated, not just periodically attacked. These are the people who go in circles of defeat, are forever oppressed, and can't ever get ahead.

This is why it is necessary to question who is in charge of the regime (or empire) so that the king pin and HIS footholds can be torn down. Look, if soldiers of a regime who've taken over your country are stationed in your home and daily implement assaults to keep you at bay and powerless but somehow you outwit them, remove them from the premises or escape, have you obtained control of your territory? Is your battle over? No. New soldiers (snakes/minions) are assigned to regain control over you and implement the next assault. This is the missing piece to the spirit of python puzzle and is sure to aid many into true freedom once and for all.

God is far superior to the spirit of python and his empire. The powers of darkness are but microscopic in scale to God and the endless sea of His majesty. Yet, Python has a grip on so many of God's children and this mystery is untangled throughout this title. It will become understood that Satan doesn't have tricks up his sleeve that have evaded God's omnipotence after all. That God really does care and hasn't just sat back and relaxed while the spirit of python has dragged His people through the mud.

By the time you have finished reading this book, I pray you will understand better what's been going on in your life and are better equipped to move forward into the plans God specifically destined for you - and out of the grip of Python.

"My people are destroyed for lack of knowledge..." Hosea 4:6 KJV. The verse is reflecting more specifically *'the knowledge of God'* but I assure you that it ties in to lacking knowledge of who our enemy is. Further, Jesus told us in John 8:32 NIV, *"Then you will know the truth, and the truth will set you free."*

Father God,

I pray that You bless all readers and guard their hearts and minds in Christ Jesus. Anoint this book so that each and every time it is read, understanding will flow and hearts will come into alignment with truth. May all receive revelation and power to rise up in Christ to overcome.

Bring everyone's mind into focus and clear out the spirits which cause confusion. I bind every hindering spirit that sets itself against this reader and God. And I ask You, Father God, to set numerous angels about the reader, Lord, and lift them, fill them with your Spirit. Open their minds to comprehend the full breadth of the truth in order to be transformed. Encourage, them, Lord, even now, that the spirits which stood so powerful against them for so long...are actually...powerless. Lead them to take a stand as they grasp the truth. Deliver them and reprogram their minds where the spirit of python would try to maintain a hold or regain entry. And finally, Father God, help them to finish the book in its entirety and bring them to complete understanding of all You want them to know and a complete comprehension of who they are in You and who You are in them. In Jesus' Mighty Name, Amen.

Chapter One
The Many Faces Of Python

It's important to establish that, according to the revelation I believe the Lord released, the spirit of python is but a surname given to a very specific general appointed under Satan to destroy the one true church. I know this is a new concept. What has been understood is the spirit of python is just one type of demonic, (specifically prophetic) worker but, based on my experiences as well as scripture and other factors, we aren't talking about one type of demon. We're talking about an empire that is responsible for the demonic workings against believers in Christ for the sake of deeming us powerless!

People are desperate to figure out how to escape the dark clouds that follow them and probably hope there's a fix-it-quick prayer or formula laid out in this book that will cause things to change swiftly. While this is certainly possible, it's more likely that the empire's secret that I aim to expose here has numerous footholds and systems in place in people. Putting it frankly, the totality of our freedom is in our oneness with Christ. And Python's empire rules every inch of us that isn't in alignment with truth so his empire is out to keep us from grasping it. And then he rules Christians through a vast empire of all sorts of specific workers that strategically work in every area of our lives to keep believers, especially "seers", powerless. Whether it's a crawling in the mud down and out desperate defeat or a casual mediocrity that goes unnoticed, believers are not walking in their destinies, the power of God, and their inheritance and this is the real issue at hand. This is the work of Python and his empire.

Again, Python is not another random hellish powerhouse of a troublemaker mixing it up with all the others just randomly asserting whatever damage he can and seeing if he can out-do his colleagues. Though it seems everyone is locked in this perspective, it is an extremely limited perception of this snake. I am convinced… Python is so much more than just a random entity that wants to ensnare you so he can ruin your finances or suffocate or kill you. There's a lot more behind why those things are happening! I have spent hours speaking on this subject with people who are at their end, trying to show that their perspective of this snake is not a singular demon type only to discern at the end of the conversation that their minds are stuck on perceiving Python as just another evil troublemaker. To them, the work of Python is one assailant that shows up periodically to wreak havoc in certain departments of their lives while the reality is there's a lot more going on. This is all a part of his strategy to KEEP people where he wants them – focusing on problematic parts – chasing this issue today, that one tomorrow. Python is cool with it because you'll just keep going in the very circles you want desperately to escape. He'll just throw the next demon into action for you to need to contend with. Just so long as you are busy not coming into the full truth and power of God. It's all a part of his strategy. He has to keep you from the big picture that will cause you to activate your inheritance!

Much to my dismay, this is what I've been witnessing ever since I began attempting to convey who Python really is. It's frustrating because I see this with certainty but find it difficult to get across. The fact is if we as individuals do not begin to see and respect the whole picture, believers dominated by Python will continue to lag. They will spend the rest of their days on earth going in circles battling the minions instead of rising above Python's agenda against them.

Please hear this with the Spirit of God in you… Python is so much more than a spiritual snake getting his jollies luring someone into sin, killing somebody off or draining their bank accounts repeatedly. It's time we realize who he really is and see that there are many thousands of demons who orchestrate the whole of this empire.

We talk of many spirits such as the spirit of witchcraft or pride, the spirit of Jezebel, or even the spirit of death, to name a few. When somebody has an ongoing issue with a particular behavior or sin, such as jealousy, for example, they are thought of as possibly having a spirit of jealousy. Jesus said to the woman with the bowed back that she was loosed from the spirit of infirmity. Likewise, Jesus commanded the deaf and mute spirit to come out of one particular boy. So, we see how demons are often named or identified according to their works or assignment.

In the mid 90's, after studying the spirit of witchcraft, it seemed that the spirit of witchcraft and later, the spirit of Jezebel were all you heard about and how prominent they were in the church. Indeed, they certainly were and still are, but I wondered if we overused the names. I'd think, "Aren't there other demons at work, too? All we're talking about is two workers. What about the others???"

Later, as the spirit of python was addressed more I witnessed its name being used for *several different types of demonic influence*. Something about this troubled me because I couldn't understand how one name, the name of a snake, no less, had connections to so many variations of influence.

Such as how God revealed to me the name of the entity coiled around my body and the reason I was trapped in poverty was "Python". Outside of what the Lord directly spoke to me at that time in 1996, however, I had no additional revelation until a decade later when God broadened my understanding to this spirit's tactics.

Suddenly, I started hearing teachings about this spirit but one person would teach concerning one thing while other teachers touched on completely different aspects. Hmmm…

I essentially asked God to clarify all this to me. After all, the spirit of pythos (python) is what is named in the Greek translation of Acts 16:16 where the woman was referred to as having a spirit of divination. Yet, I heard ministers teaching how the spirit of python is much like the natural python in the way it conquers its prey by constriction - and that the enemy does this to believers by luring them into sin for the purpose of destroying them. Meanwhile, I'd had a personal encounter with God a decade earlier concerning a curse of poverty where the Holy Spirit referred to what I saw in a vision as being a python. But what did all these have to do with each other? Was the woman with the spirit of divination in Acts 16 being constricted or isolated? And why wasn't she under a curse of poverty if she was under the influence of the spirit of python like I was? It wasn't adding up so I searched God for understanding. How could one spirit be the author of so many different forms of demonic workings in people's lives? Aren't there more definitive 'names' for the specific nature of the individual types of attacks or influence? Why not just call the spirit of divination the "spirit of divination", the spirit of isolation the "spirit of isolation", and the curse of poverty that was over my life the "curse of poverty"? I wasn't getting how all the faces of python amounted to being named one single spirit. Again, one python spirit suffocates by oppressing someone while another spirit of python is devouring someone's finances while another foretells the future???

So, I began researching the spirit of python's origin and it all came together in a most extraordinary way. It's simple yet so profound! The truth is the spirit of python is actually a namesake the false prophet took on (who is actually the counterfeit equivalent of the Holy Spirit) due to ancient practices and belief systems. Through the ages, the devil has been operating via an expansive platform but the spirit of python (the counterfeit holy spirit) actually oversees a vast system of demons working from that platform together for a single, unified agenda. And while there are in fact specific spirits such as witchcraft - which the spirit of python (false prophet) employs - the spirit of python is the overseer of the entire operation. Such as the spirit of Jezebel. I will show that this spirit is under the headship of the empire set up by the python spirit. So, even though the lesser minions who have other names are the ones implementing Python's orders, we refer to the lot of them as Python.

It's like if John Doe is in the U.S. military and is overseas and personally encounters the enemy, even if they discover his name, he's more than likely still referred to by the enemy as "the American." That's what we do when we don't know the specific name - we refer to them according to their group or classification. I believe this is why all the demons who are assigned to implement the false prophet's agenda are referred to as the spirit of python. One might be a spirit of self-loathing (knew him personally) while another might be the spirit of religion while yet another is the spirit of Jezebel. But if we haven't been given the specific demon's identity and if these demons are working within the system of "Operation Python", we will naturally classify them all as the python spirit.

If this is too difficult to swallow, consider things further... The Lord gave me the vision of the snake coiled around my body and said it was responsible for the curse of poverty that was over me. Was the snake poverty itself? Or was the snake the one who influenced the circumstances to keep me in poverty?

Concerning the curse of poverty, God didn't show me a vision of my hands bound in chains despite the fact that everything I put my hands to was cursed. He didn't show me a visual of being blocked by walls of interference which I had often felt were around me as I would try to get a job and such. Those would have been accurate visions as to how the spirits kept me in poverty. But the Lord wasn't showing me a vision to confirm the curse of poverty or even to demonstrate their procedures. No. God was showing me who was in charge. He showed the python coiled around me because He wanted me to eventually figure out that it was via the false prophet that all the curses were being implemented against me. But we'll explain this later.

Now, add that to something that happened a decade later where the Lord spoke to me that the reason I had been mistreated in the various ways by other believers (rejected, belittled, falsely accused) wasn't because they were bad Christians but because the spirit of python was working to keep me isolated. The spirit of python? But it was the spirit of rejection working in the one scenario, it was a condescending spirit in another, and an accusing spirit in another situation. These were all unique assaults yet the Lord classified them as the spirit of python. Why?

This was merely the beginning of my understanding. I didn't start to put it all together until 2009 when I looked into the origin of the python spirit. That's when it all made sense and when I realized why the Lord kept naming the various demonic influences as Python.

<u>Things To Consider</u>

How many faces has the spirit of python used to hinder your life?

Chapter Review Checkpoints

1. What are aspects of the spirit of python we know to be taught today?

A) he is the divination spirit operating in the woman of Acts 16
B) he constricts and suffocates his prey much like the natural python
C) he hinders our ability to worship God
D) he interferes with our finances
E) he lures people into isolation
F) he hinders our ability to read the Word of God
G) he hinders our ability to pray
H) he hinders our ambition and hope
I) all of the above and more

2. Python might accomplish suffocating and hindering us in all the above ways through tactics like rejection, low self-esteem, tragedy, abuse, financial devastation, continual loss and injustice, etc. But aren't these the workings of other spirits who have their own names?
   Yes or No

3. Based on the above, is it not necessary to raise the question as to how one entity is given credit for the many faces behind these works?
   Yes or No

ANSWER KEY - CHAPTER II
1-I, 2-Y, 3-Y

Chapter Two

Signs That Python Has A Grip

Everyone in the world will experience some or all of the following at some point or another. But when many of these things occur repeatedly and are the norm, especially in the life of a believer who knows and has access to the Power of ALL powers, Christ Jesus, then it's highly probable Python's empire is running the show. And while his signature boils down to stifling their connection to God's power, the following *ongoing* traits of someone's life are pronounced indicators that Python has a solid grip:

Lethargy, Sluggishness	Isolation	Hopelessness
Poverty	Frequent Letdowns	Striving but Struggling
Peculiar Financial Setbacks	Few Quality Relationships	No Fruit to Major Efforts
Constriction/Suffocation	Dark Clouds Hovering	Foggy minded
Difficulty Focusing	Weariness	Lack of Ambition
Feeling Paralyzed	Indifference	Apathy
Opression	Suicidal Thoughts	Depression
Frequent Defeat	Difficulty Worshiping	Difficulty Praying

This list is most likely incomplete. The best way to determine that something is a sign that Python has a grip is by considering if the stifling nature of the occurrences are ongoing, if they keep them from moving forward or experiencing victory in life; and above all else, they keep them from their inheritance and authority in Christ.

Keep in mind, the traits are evidence of his dominion, *not his end goal*. That is the reason I believe the Lord wants this book written. Thus far, teachings only disclose how Python gets in, how he wants to destroy, as though this is his bottom line. Not here. This title urges readers to realize the "why" behind Python's agenda so to equip people from not only coming out of his influence but INTO God's plan – the very thing he wants to stop! I perceive that folks look on these symptoms as though they (and the "snake" behind it) are what needs fixed or removed. This makes sense but the Lord wants people to realize there's more to it than just getting free from these problems. God wants His children to realize they were destined to be powerful to the defeating of such darkness and (because this is not understood) this is *why* the darkness rages against them.

God also wants people to realize their goal should not be to seek to get out of Python's grip *for their own sake*, but *for God's sake* so they can do the powerful things God wants them to. And last, God wants people to realize the reason Python even *has* a grip is because they are unaware of some or a lot of His truths, who they are in Him, and Who He is in them… Father God wants His children to come into oneness with Christ which is the **ONLY** way Python will lose his ability to effect and rule them. There's no other way. True unity with Christ deems Python **POWERLESS**!!!

That is the bottom line to this book. Python isn't only a troublemaker you need rid of, He's an empire that Christ put under your feet over 2000 years ago and you just have to discover this fact.

If you are a seer, called to ministry, called to workings of miracles, called to power in Christ, you have a relentless empire set in place to try to hold you down.

That's why your goal here and now should no longer be to try to figure out how to get rid of the trouble maker and see all your problems resolved but to come into Christ with all Your heart, soul, mind, and strength where it is no longer POSSIBLE for Python to rule.

However, if you are still looking for a simpler solution, something like deliverance training or a 30 hour exorcism session to rid you of Python's reign in your life, you won't find it here. Not that there isn't a place for these somewhere in your life. There may be. Deliverance from strongholds (false programming, mindsets, deep rooted deceptions) must happen and there will hopefully be plenty of them broken via the revelations brought forth in this title. Because deliverance happens by knowing the truth. Christ's holy truth cuts through the deceptions bit by bit and delivers us. Then exorcisms, or the casting out of demons, are for when demons are possessing someone. But casting demons out does not rid one of the exterior empire which strategizes against us. Nor does it exorcise your anointing or calling away which makes you their target. You will remain a threat to the dark kingdom as long as you are on earth so Python's empire will continue to target you from the outside even after demons are expelled. His empire doesn't only rule you by possessing you, he rules you by distressing you through other people, interference in your finances, your circumstances, etc. Remember, his goal is to implement whatever it takes shut you down and drive you to your defeated grave. And your only protection from it is being one with the truth and the way.

Applications & Strategies Python Employs

The strategies Python uses (even subtly) to get people where he wants them – **powerless** – are diverse. And his number one underlying tactic is to keep God's children busy wrapped up in or striving against the following types of orchestrated issues:

Hurt / Anger / Bitterness / Self Pity / Depression
(via inundations of rejections, injustice, violations, abuse)

Idolatry
(love or compulsion for or addiction to sex, drugs, entertainment, materialism, success, reputation)

Loneliness
(by keeping them isolated or damaging all relationships so they never have quality ones or healthy support systems; forever preoccupied with how alone they are)

Weariness / Sluggishness / Apathy / Lethargy towards life
(via sickness, by tearing down our stamina via poor nutrition, lack of exercise, or being toxic;
or overworking to death while getting nowhere)

Defeat / Hopelessness
(via persistent setbacks, injustice, heartbreaks, let downs, nothing ever working out)

Inferiority / Insecurity / Low Self View / Shame
(via a life of criticism, abuse, abandonment, mockery, condescension, being an outcast, a disappointment, never properly loved, never believed in, valued, affirmed)

It seems I have just described the rampant conditions of the entire world…. TA-DA! Okay, no need to be snide but simply to show that these issues and the demons behind them should not individually remain as the focus! Because they ALL serve a unified, global agenda. Regardless of which applications work against you and which work against another, the end result is Satan wants everyone (spiritually) powerless and it's the false prophet's job to accomplish this.

You might say it sounds like I'm making Python out to be the devil himself. No. As you'll see in the following chapters, Satan, in his goal to becoming 'god' over all the earth (which he is soon to accomplish) has two generals. They are the spirit of antichrist and the counter of the Holy Spirit which is the false prophet. These two are behind the infiltration of evil into all the aspects of life. I believe the spirit of antichrist's responsibility is to corrupt, pollute, twist, and break down the economy, education and government. The counter of the Holy Spirit's responsibility is to attack religion and faith; to point the way to false gods and away from God and his power. To pollute the truth, the church, to deem her powerless. So together, as the false prophet stifles God's power which helps the spirit of antichrist gain momentum in the running of the world, they will eventually usher in their father, Satan.

The way Python implements the above strategies is by working through all sorts of people starting at our births to do their bidding. And sadly, everyone is capable of being a tool. I've seen the most precious people used in an attempt to attack a person of God. Including family and loved ones.

And now here's why all these strategies work for Python... People with a lot of these elements in their history are programmed to doubt God's love and the reality that He is a good God and that He cares for us. The empire uses these as much as he can get away with to condition people to feel God is beyond their reach, is lost in space, is negligent, absent, uncaring, is fed up with them, and often times... *that God is the one allowing or doing all the horrible things to them!* These people to one degree or another are trained to have confidence in the bad as opposed to good. That way, when the day comes that they give their lives to Jesus, there are severe, deep soul programs in place that continue to quietly run even while these new believers earnestly follow God's ways. They know the Bible says Jesus loves them so they choose to believe it. But it's only a head belief, they don't actually comprehend it or relate deep down. And they genuinely give themselves over to Christianity; perhaps even to service and daily attention to God's Word and prayer expecting that their new ways of right living will bring them into the promises of God which are good. Only to find the same dark clouds still hovering at every turn.

These clouds remain because though the new believer was born of Spirit and has a reverence and a measure of love for God, their subconscious perception of God is skewed and they don't realize a part of them is falsely programmed and operating accordingly. That while on one hand the intention is for righteousness, on the other, there are many lies secretly impeding it. The LIFE of the Spirit of God in them is in conflict with the hidden insecurities (strongholds/bondage) that remain. Their newfound faith is trying to rise, but their faith in what always was is secretly, even subconsciously, working against it.

The false prophet knows that your not being aware that God is enthusiastically on your side, that He has a tremendously wonderful plan for you, that He really doesn't like all the crap that happened to you... is how he maintains his place in your life. And the fact is that not being convinced that God is passionately in love with you regardless of how the world has treated you..... is believing everything the devil told you which means he has ground in you. Not to mention, the power you believe is the power you release to manifest in your life. Python knows this, that's why he had to inundate you since your youth to condition you to have confidence in his lies over God's love and truth.

"Well, if God is so great and loving and powerful, why didn't He do something about it and not let the enemy program me to not know His love?" There's a pretty extensive answer to that but in a nutshell, it all boils down to legality and free will. It's up to us to seek out and become one with the truth and the Almighty One. God will not manipulate anything to have His way – which is that we choose Him and spend eternity with Him. He set it into place that we have to choose for ourselves. Period.

    It's unfortunate for us that we were all born in a day and hour where the enemy has infiltrated the things of earth so thoroughly that the amazing truths of God are obscure even if we are raised in the church. But that's just how it is. It's more difficult to see and comprehend the complete reality of the living God now than it ever was all through time. But this doesn't change the fact that Father God made the way through Christ and left it up to us to not only find Christ, but to let Christ come alive in us so that we would overcome the world indeed. Most of us stop at "finding Christ". We get cozy with mediocre Christianity and fail to earnestly seek and practice the fullness of the inheritance He handed to us on a silver platter. And for those of us who are anointed to do great things IN Christ, especially if we are seers or have the gift of miracles and such, it is to our detriment to not pursue the all of Christ with fervency because we are therefore enabling the spirit of Python to take our breath and keep us powerless. We are allowing Python to derail us from our destinies of authority and blessing. Yes, we are the ones allowing it.

    This doesn't mean there's no compassion for the pain of what the empire has put some of us through because it's all horrible. But once we understand how it was all a part of the big plan and strategy and then identify the holes in our souls where Python's doorways are, where he rules, we can begin to disalign ourselves with the lies and false programs so that the LIFE of CHRIST in us takes over and we begin to soar in our alignment with Glory!

The bottom line is that when the spirit of Python has prominent ground in anyone's life, including and especially the believer's, he is successful at:

a) keeping us from praying and worshiping
b) putting out our fire for God
c) luring us into isolation
d) causing us to 'feel' hopeless and defeated
e) trapping us in poverty or hindering us from prospering
f) luring us into self destructive behaviors or lifestyles - suicide
g) causing us to doubt or not comprehend God's personal love for us
h) causing us to doubt the Word of God and the promises He has for us
i) causing us to be ineffective for Christ - loss of anointing
j) keeping us going in circles, getting nowhere with life
k) causing us to feel lethargic, indifferent, and apathetic about life or God
l) causing us to always feel rejected and violated, etc.
m) causing us to feel small, inadequate, incapable, inferior, insecure
n) causing us to walk by fear and not by faith, leaning on our own understanding
o) causing divisions in the body of Christ and marriages
p) thwarting or delaying us from walking in our purpose and call
q) dominating us via the hurts, bitterness, and pain that he heaped on us
r) keeping us wrapped up in our problems and less attentive to others & God
s) convincing us that God doesn't care or that it's His fault our lives are a mess
t) etc.

Just who is this mega spirit called Python that we've come to know so well?

AGAIN:
HE IS THE FALSE PROPHET
aka: The Counterfeit Holy Spirit

What? He's not supposed to come on the scene until the end when the Antichrist takes bodily form! Wrong! These two beasts which are spoken of in Revelations 12 and 13 have been here all along – in spirit and with a hardcore agenda. The Lord showed me that just as the spirit of antichrist has been infiltrating the systems of earth since the Garden of Eden, the false prophet has had a prominent role, too!

Satan counterfeits ALL that God does, so if the first beast in Revelations is the spirit of antichrist which is the counterfeit of the true Christ, then, you got it... the second beast must be the counterfeit of the Holy Spirit!

Now consider this: What are all the characteristics and 'jobs' of the Holy Spirit in our lives? Next, ponder for just a moment... that if there were a Holy Spirit **COUNTERFEIT**, would he not have the complete opposite characteristics and 'jobs'? Would he not be on a mission to imitate all the Holy Spirit does but in a dark way that pulls us away from truth instead of INTO truth where the Holy Spirit is always guiding us? Let's take a look at what our precious Holy Spirit does and then contrast it with what the counterfeit does.

The Holy Spirit VS The Counterfeit

H) Points the way to Christ – draws us to God and righteousness

C) Points the way to false gods, false religion, idolatry, luring us away from God

H) Is the Comforter, brings a glorious peace we sometimes can't explain

C) Promotes FALSE comforts in self, success, idolatry, independence, addiction, etc

H) Guides us towards right living, truth, our purpose and destiny

C) Guides us via deception into destructive lifestyles and away from our purpose

H) Endows whom He pleases with HOLY spiritual gifts and power for the edification of the body and deliverance of the world from darkness

C) Endows whom he pleases with false powers (sorcery, witchcraft, voodoo) for the tearing down and destruction of the body and cementing the world in darkness

H) Gives divine HOLY utterance (via tongues or words through the prophets) which promote life, unity, truth, destiny, hope, righteousness

C) Gives FALSE utterance (psychics, diviners, unsuspecting or prideful saints) which promote wickedness, death, destruction, division, loss, hopelessness

H) Unveils/illuminates/reveals the mysteries of scripture to those born of God in Spirit

C) Veils the truth of scripture - does everything to keep us from the Word of God via distractions, oppression, confusion or mental fogginess, sickness, lethargy and apathy, busyness with life, idolatry, worldliness

H) Lifts us up, lightens, puts a spring back into our step, refreshes, invigorates

C) Weighs people down, depletes them, wears them out, oppresses

H) Convicts us of sin - Compels us to return to holiness

C) Promotes, undermines, waters down sin - says it's okay

H) Directs us through dreams & visions which train, equip, or lead us into our purpose

C) Thwarts the direction God wants us to walk in by luring us down wrong paths

H) Gives divine revelation, wisdom, knowledge, etc. which promotes Holy Kingdom truths and blesses the body and the world

C) Gives FALSE revelations, false wisdom which promotes wickedness, dark agendas and leads us into deep despair and farther from God

H) Authors miracles, healings & blessings which solidify/demonstrate God's love and truth

C) Steals miracles and healings and thwarts blessings to make God look like a liar or like He doesn't love us as He truly does. Performs false miracles to validate false agenda

H) Breathes life into us which empowers us to FULL LIFE!

C) Suffocates us in order to shorten, delay, or destroy our lives.

HOW ARE THE COUNTERFEIT AND PYTHON ONE IDENTITY?

All the signs that Python has dominion discussed earlier outline the very things the counterfeit of the Holy Spirit would do to UNDO and DISMANTLE the work of the Holy Spirit - to take the very power, breath and life Holy Spirit breathed into us! Therefore, is it not obvious? The spirit of Python IS the counter of our glorious Holy Spirit!

Again, we have only been addressing the spirit of python as just another minion like witchcraft. And (please hear this) this is how the false prophet wants it to stay! Because that way we continue just plucking out the splinters instead of getting out of Splinter City altogether! We keep busy tearing down minions instead of dethroning the high prince!

Everything, EVERYTHING that has ever happened to stifle you in any way is of the spirit of python (the counterfeit of the Holy Spirit) and his very singular agenda is to run you into the ground in order to deem you powerless for Christ. This is the missing link in all the teaching about the spirit of python. We have yet to appreciate that it's about more than causing good people trouble just because... It's for the ultimate purpose of keeping power from rising up in the earth that will hinder Satan's plan to become god.

Are you a seer? Do you feel called to ministry? This is why Python had to secure a throne deep within you and why he gets away with hindering your life no matter what you try and despite your walk with Jesus. You are called of God to walk in power; you were chosen for such a time as this. You are, therefore, a prime target. Python has been striving to keep you from coming into your destiny. His primary job is to protect his father's kingdom by keeping God's power in the world mute. If you are anointed, you are a threat. Why would he just kick back and watch as you blossom in power and glory through Christ? Do you understand he isn't just causing trouble because of mere gratification of destruction? He's causing trouble that will keep you impotent! Decide right now that you need much more than to get Python out of your life, you need to realize he's kept you from your destiny! Change your objective from trying to get rid of this troublemaker to coming in to WHO YOU ARE in Christ.

Things To Consider

Do you understand better now why it is important to grasp who Python really is?

Chapter Review Checkpoints

1. If you have relentlessly experienced many of the signs and symptoms of Python's grip most of your life, it is because

    A) you are called to walk in the power of God which would do damage to the dark kingdom
    B) Python is keeping you busy striving and struggling in order to divert you from your destiny in Christ
    C) you are a target because of your anointing and potential to promote the Kingdom of God and His power in the earth
    D) all of the above

2. It is imperative that we understand who Python really is so that we change our objective from merely escaping his influence to coming in to the fullness of our inheritance in Christ for the sake of God's Kingdom.

   T or F

3. Python does not want you to understand that he is the counterfeit of the Holy Spirit because he needs you to continue striving against the issues.

   T or F

ANSWER KEY - CHAPTER II
1-D, 2-T, 3-T

Chapter Three
The Beginning Of A Dark Kingdom

Let's begin by establishing the bottom line of the devil's agenda. Note, I said 'devil' and not the spirit of python. This is because Python is merely the name given to the vast platform we are discussing in this book but behind every platform of darkness is the same prince; satan. And before we can appreciate any given platform, we really need to get a solid grip on Satan's overall agenda.

It's no mystery…Satan opposes God and seeks to be the god of heaven and earth. But despite being the prince of the air after being cast out of heaven and down to earth, without a platform to work through in the natural "material" realm of the earth, he had no kingdom! Oh, he had a company of demons. But who did he have to rule? Nobody. So, therefore, no kingdom. But it wouldn't remain this way for long.

We know the story quite well where Satan tempted Eve in the Garden of Eden which brought sin into the world but do we understand the depth of how and what he accomplished here? The truth of his identity was that he had no rights in the earth because man was the one who was granted dominion over it. Man was the possessor. Satan was merely present and wandering with no platform; no authority. So, if he wanted a platform through which to operate in the natural, he'd have to establish it through mankind, hence, his trickery in the Garden.

This was how Satan launched his kingdom. Yes, Adam and Eve's disobedience in the Garden is widely understood as 'the fall of man' and is why sin is now our nature. But while these are the results of sin entering our realm and certainly do require our attention, this wasn't all that was on the devil's mind. You see, since his goal was to rule that which God created he would have to infiltrate the natural kingdom to set up a supernatural kingdom within it.

Prior to the introduction of sin, Satan was dominant over absolutely nothing nor did he hold a preeminent position whatsoever! But watch how the devil cleverly runs for governor in Eve's life, wins her vote, and then together with her husband, they sign him into office.

Somehow, after studying her, Satan identified what it would take to engage Eve and bring her into a place of agreement or submission to him. Note that when the serpent approached Eve he did not straight up say, "Hey you, I command you to eat of that forbidden fruit." He couldn't command her to disobey God; Eve had to come to the decision on her own. Satan didn't bring up the specific tree of knowledge at all, rather, he posed a question that sent Eve's thinking into a path of questioning God. And note the way he posed the question: "Did God really say, 'You must not eat from any tree in the garden'?" (Genesis 3:1 NIV). God never said that! Satan is clearly promoting rebellion by suggesting Eve should ponder what God did or did not say. When he succeeded and she was submissive in thought, which became evident in her explaining to the devil what God did say and then listening to his suggestion that God was holding back on them, Eve then proceeded further in thought to determine to eat the forbidden fruit. Satan never told her to do it. He merely, but cleverly, guided her thought process to decide it for herself. She apparently never had a problem with whether or not 'God was holding back on them' before. But somehow Satan detected that if he caressed her thoughts just the right way she would choose to agree - and he was correct. We see how he successfully engaged Eve in considering her options by sending her mind into that particular rebellious flow of thought.

The definition of "kingdom" in the Merriam-Webster Dictionary is: a) *a realm or region in which something is dominant;* or b) *an area or sphere in which one holds a preeminent position.*

Now, here's something to ponder... We think the eating of the forbidden fruit is what brought sin into the world because it was an act of disobedience to God. This is certainly true but is only HALF of the sin equation because disobeying God at the temptation of the enemy is, likewise, obeying the devil. And this is significant because that which we obey is where our allegiance is. Sin is, therefore, an agreement, an alignment or even a conjoining with darkness. That which we obey which is indicated by our actions is what we are in covenant with. Satan understood this very well and needed to bring man into agreement with him. But not in thought alone. Adam had to show his agreement via his actions which would bring him into contractual unity with the devil. This, thereby, would provide the approval the liar needed to acquire legal ground and usher the nature of sin into our realm and ultimately, Satan's government.

Incidentally, I don't believe Eve alone could have given Satan the platform. Had Adam resisted his wife and forbade her from eating the forbidden fruit or at least not ate of it himself, the entire fall of man and Satan's kingdom being established in our realm might have been thwarted because Adam was the head over Eve. Satan needed Adam's signature ultimately. But this is just my theory.

At any rate, the devil, a spiritual entity only, a non-physical being, needed man (a spiritual and physical being in one who had dominion over the earth) to agree with him in order to gain viable entry into our physical realm. But that agreement had to be backed by their signature which was their obedience to the suggestion that they had options, hence, eating of the forbidden fruit. Satan knew his ticket to having a platform on earth, or more clearly his ticket to building his dark, spiritual kingdom in the earth, meant causing the humans who did dominate the earth to step outside of the governance of the only kingdom they had known with God. Up to that point, Satan could only talk a good game - but never could he play it because he was supernatural while man was natural and ruled over all that was natural. The serpent could only tempt the natural realm but not manifest his powers unless a connection or agreement, medium, or platform was established between him and man. So, when Eve and then Adam ate the forbidden fruit, they were in agreement with the liar whereby his nature (evil/sin) infiltrated the natural realm. Sin, then, became the platform and "right-of-way" through which the devil could implement and manifest his powers and government of his new found kingdom.

But was Satan's goal simply to be god to people here and there and figured the more, the merrier? No. Let's comprehend that Satan's goal has always been to be the god of ALL the earth. Isaiah 14:12-14 KJV declares, "How art thou fallen from heaven, O Lucifer, son of the morning! how art thou cut down to the ground, which didst weaken the nations! For thou hast said in thine heart, I will ascend into heaven, I will exalt my throne above the stars of God: I will sit also upon the mount of the congregation, in the sides of the north: I will ascend above the heights of the clouds; I will be like the most High."

This is Satan's very passion and mission. He, therefore, has had to work earnestly, diligently and strategically at mastering all the souls of earth in order to 'ascend above the heights of the clouds and be like the most High'. He has to cause it that his kingdom, which started out void of power, I repeat, *void of power*, continues to deceive and bring man into agreement with the governance of his kingdom (through their minds just as it was with Eve), so that his kingdom swells in power and grows to the point of taking over every nation as a whole in the earth. (Does this smell something like a one world order?)

This is pretty serious if we take the time to grasp it. The enemy is not only very real, but very, very active. He's got an astronomical agenda. He's on a mission to take over the world. And since his power is only a reality in our natural realm when we give him ground, he is working feverishly to bring us into agreement with him so that he gains ground. We've been giving control of this world to an evil entity who is simply powerless without our consent. And we're so blind to it...

You know... There has to be a certain perverted type of glory Satan feels as he rules entire nations and dominates the hearts of the lives of a higher number of souls than the Mighty God has for centuries. There must be a great sense of satisfaction when he's got entire cultures wrapped around his finger practicing ideals that are twisted and contrary to the heart of God. There must be even greater glory perceived in seeing how successful he is at hindering and even suffocating the believers in the God of Abraham, Isaac, and Jacob. He also has a great deal to pride himself on in the authoring of countless false religions or atheistic views to which more people submit than the number who submit to Jesus Christ.

Are we getting the picture? This is the drive of the prince of the air and ruler of darkness. This is his singular mission. Satan launched his kingdom in the Garden of Eden and has been strategically working towards taking over the earth ever since that moment. Since then, he has literally conquered nations and rules countless hearts with a vengeance. He laughs in mockery at the foolishness of men who so easily bow to his every suggestion and self-serving ideologies; who are so gullible and weak to recognize the absurdity of the falsities he lays before them. He even mocks God saying how stupid God was to give dominion over to dust in the first place. He sneers at governments and leaders who hold their heads high because of their power while many of them are merely puppets controlled by his own hand. But he sits back and allows them to bask in their glory because he knows that he's the one who's really in control of these nations. Yes, the nations of the earth dedicated to ideals contrary to God are literally under the governance of Satan's kingdom and he calls these physical kingdoms... his. Look at how he said to Jesus in Matthew 4:8-9 NIV, "Again, the devil took him to a very high mountain and showed him all the kingdoms of the world and their splendor. 'All this I will give you'," he said, "'if you will bow down and worship me'."

How it is this prince who was at one time void of possessing anything on earth is now in the position to offer kingdoms to God Himself as though they are his to offer? Clearly, it's because they were! He knew he had legitimate authority over them! He ruled those kingdoms spiritually and still does! They were given over to him by man's agreeing with his policies and adopting his ideals. Mankind, whether wittingly or not, elected Satan as Prince of the air. His kingdom was the spiritual authority ruling over the very earthly kingdoms he offered Christ Jesus. He would NOT have been able to offer the kingdoms to Jesus had man not been submitting to Satan's government and placed him in authority. He did not have them simply because he existed; he acquired them through deception and man's submission to him.

Colossians 1:13-14 NIV says, "For (Father God) has rescued us from the dominion of darkness and brought us into the kingdom of the Son he loves, in whom we have redemption, the forgiveness of sins." And in Luke 11:18 NIV, Jesus says, "If Satan also be divided against himself, how shall his kingdom stand?" Clearly, this entity who doesn't have to be anything more than a footstool to us instead is a mighty kingdom.

We must comprehend that there are two very real and mighty spiritual kingdoms and EVERYONE participates in either of them at any given point in our thought processes, our speaking, our motives, our moods, how we treat others, how we react, in the choices we make, and in the actions we take. All these will reflect whether we are in compliance with Holy Kingdom government, or the policies of hell. In one moment we might be operating according to God's policies. But what about the next?

The fact that Satan has a kingdom is no grand revelation to most. Yet, for some reason, we don't appreciate its reality or how prominent in our world it is. It is foolish to argue this point because the fact is if we did grasp it entirely, we'd have been better on the alert watching and discerning how we might be making way for darkness to reign over us. We further don't comprehend the magnitude of influence his kingdom has or we'd be careful to not fall prey to it so easily. Yet, we don't. Here we are, many of us.... Going in circles, defeated at times in one arena or another and wandering in the wilderness aimlessly crying, "What is going on?" We undermine and are so passive concerning the powerful role the kingdom of darkness plays in our world. I mean, think about it. When you read earlier where I said how Satan has his own kingdom and he wants to take over the world, you probably weren't shocked and reacting with, "Oh my gosh, he does???" Because you already knew it. Yet, what have we done about it? Do we respect this cold, harsh reality? Has knowing this compelled us to most assuredly hide under the shadow of the Almighty. Nah... It's a situation of 'out of sight, out of mind'. Besides, we're too busy figuring out our lives or mastering our 'selves' or being religious or even 'anti' religious.

Our response to the reality that the devil has a powerful kingdom through which he wants to rule over earth should be, "Oh my gosh, he does!!! And it's time we hide under the shadow of the Almighty so that HIS (The Almighty God's) Kingdom is the one we are bowing down and submitting to. So that HIS Kingdom is the one ruling POWERFULLY over, in, and through our lives AND our nations."

The bottom line is the government principles we agree with and walk in establishes who we give legal authority to. Being born again rescues us from the devil's ability to maintain the dominion he deceptively acquired in our lives but we have to personally reject his dominion by getting out of his territory. Jesus gave us the key to escape the devil's prison but if we don't walk out of the prison by disconnecting from the dark government, we choose to remain in the devil's territory where he can continue to rule over us.

We have been granted entrance to the Holy Kingdom! The problem is so few of us think we've only been granted a 'get out of hell free' card. Yet, even now, while still walking the earth, we have access to all that the Holy Kingdom offers! But we have to walk in and abide by the Holy Kingdom government in order to partake of its wondrous benefits. Likewise, we must reject every single aspect of the dark kingdom government (like sin - big and little, wrong mental programming, idolatry, selfishness, pride, unforgiveness, hate, doubting God, covetousness, etc.) in order to relinquish the devil's legal right to continue ruling in our lives.

Things To Consider

Where and how might you still be in agreement with and operating in dark government policies?

Chapter Review Checkpoints

1. Satan ushered sin into the natural realm by deceiving Eve in the Garden of Eden because he:

> A. Needed to establish a platform through which to operate in the natural realm
>
> B. Needed a way to kick start the dark kingdom
>
> C. Wanted to take over the world
>
> D. All of the above

2. Satan's power was effective against man and earth

> A. The moment he utilized the serpent to do his bidding
>
> B. The moment Eve began pondering his suggestive leading
>
> C. Only after he acquired man's submission to him by their agreeing with him which was demonstrated by their actions
>
> D. Since the moment he was cast out of Heaven to the earth.

3. The devil has had one primary agenda above all else, and it has been

    A. To kill, steal, and destroy

    B. To take over the world

    C. To take as many people away from God as he possibly can

    D. To infiltrate the earth with as much wickedness and sin as possible

4. Satan has a very real and active kingdom but as long as we don't practice Satan worship or witchcraft or anything having to do with the occult, he cannot influence our lives.
    T or F

5. The devil has to acquire our signature (or agreement with him which is demonstrated in our actions) before having legal ability to influence our lives.
    T or F

6. The devil lost all legal access to man when Christ died and rose again.
    T or F

7. Disobeying God at the temptation of the devil is obeying the devil.
    T or F

8. Choosing to sin is our way of agreeing with, submitting to, and coming into covenant with the kingdom of darkness. But only if it is MAJOR sin. T or F

9. We, as a Christian body at large, need to realize that the devil is feverishly trying to maintain legal rights and control over our lives.
T or F

10. The bottom line is Satan was void of power until we agreed with him.
T or F

11. Being born again rescues us from the devil's ability to maintain the dominion he deceptively acquired in our lives but we have to personally reject his dominion by renouncing our agreements and getting out of his territory.
T or F

12. Jesus gave us the key to escape the devil's prison but if we don't walk out of the prison by disconnecting from dark government policies, we choose to remain in the devil's territory where he can continue to rule over us.
T or F

ANSWER KEY - CHAPTER III
1-D, 2-C, 3-B, 4-F, 5-T, 6-F 7-T, 8-F, 9-T, 10-T, 11-T, 12-T

Chapter Four
Understanding The Kingdoms

We are about to unravel the mysteries of the spirit of python but first, it is important to discuss the dynamics of the supernatural kingdoms.

We understand natural kingdoms to be systems of government where standards, rules and regulations are implemented. A king or queen (or other leading officials depending on the type of government) decides these boundaries and it is understood that failure to comply with the governing rules subjects one to consequences set into motion by that same system of government.

Since the fall of man, the natural kingdom of earth life has had a set of dynamics or "rules" in place that even without added influence from the dark kingdom, there is decay, decline, deterioration, and depreciation. In fact, it takes great effort for man to maintain life and even more to cause it to improve or increase. Consider the body and how it ages and declines automatically. One can work their body in such a way as to prolong or increase the value of their life, but the general decline of the body is inevitable. It's the same with every other aspect of life on earth and we accept it as normal because it is what it is.

But there is no such decay, decline, deterioration, or depreciation in the Kingdom of God! None! So, when Jesus walked among us in the natural realm and announced that the Kingdom of God is upon us, he was introducing that the glory dynamics of His divine realm were now accessible to the earth bound. Then He secured our access to them through His shed blood and we were amazingly able to partake of the realm of glory while still residing in the realm of decay.

How much we do this is up to us, of course. Many believers, unfortunately, fail to get to know God well enough to realize the wonder that's at our fingertips. We are comfortable with the normalcy of the natural kingdom of life and anticipate that glory is only accessible upon our departing from the earth realm.

There is another mighty kingdom at work within the natural realm of earth called darkness. Where, sadly, the more we approve of and practice the principles of that evil kingdom, the more the destructive dynamics of that kingdom legally impact our lives. The more we experience loss, oppression, destruction and every other kind of evil that only comes from that kingdom. Unfortunately, we are so accustomed to the influx of darkness in the natural realm that we accept it as normal as well!

Thankfully, the Lord our God made it possible to defeat the dark kingdom by providing our reconciliation to Him through Jesus but then also providing the Word and the Holy Spirit for us to hide ourselves in while still on the earth. The Word of God provides the written statutes and dynamics of glory's government. The Word is divine LIFE eternal. When you love God with all your heart you will instinctively seek to discover Him through His written Word and will gradually be transformed into the light and power that the Word is. The more we become one with His Word by the help of the Holy Spirit, the more we inherit the glory of the Kingdom of God. And the more the glorious LIFE of God is unleashed into us.

I have always been taken with the scripture verses that speak about the Kingdom of God. When I saw those three words, "Kingdom of God", I immediately associated them with Heaven.

But as I became more familiar with scripture, I began to recognize that the "Kingdom of God" wasn't Heaven rather, it was about Heaven's governmental system and dynamics.

Consider how in Matthew 12:28 NLT (and also in Luke 11:20) Jesus says, "But if I am casting out demons by the Spirit of God, then the Kingdom of God has arrived among you." Did that mean Heaven arrived? Did the streets of gold and the pearly gates of Heaven suddenly replace the city streets and gates of Jerusalem? No. Rather, the manifestation and/or power of Heaven's governmental dynamics were on the scene because where the Holy Spirit is, where Jesus is, the Kingdom of God is - which is where things happen not according to our limited understanding and nature, but according to Heavenly, supernatural dynamics.

The Kingdom of God arriving among us in Matthew 12 provides us a magnificent and beautiful reality to embrace. Typically, no government can show up and implement authority in another territorial jurisdiction. Clearly, the physical realm had its governing authorities in place and even Jesus, the Son of Man, was subject to those authorities and humbly submitted himself unto them. But the spiritual authorities legally ruling over the territory (as established in Matthew 4:8) was Satan. So how was it Jesus could exercise any spiritual authority? How could He override the legal spiritual government that mankind put into place via submission? The answer is poetically illustrated in Matthew 12:28-29 where Jesus continues,

"But if I am casting out demons by the Spirit of God, then the Kingdom of God has arrived among you. For who is powerful enough to enter the house of a strong man like Satan and plunder his goods? Only someone even stronger—someone who could tie him up and then plunder his house." NLT.

Ha!

But every time I ever hear that scripture referenced, the speakers are always emphasizing the point that first we must bind satan before we can plunder him. While this is certainly significant, the more profound point I believe

Jesus was making was He is the SUPERIOR Kingdom. One kingdom cannot bind, plunder and take over a neighboring kingdom unless it is the stronger of the two! One King can't just waltz into another kingdom and start calling the shots without either taking it over or establishing his superiority - if he indeed has it. Jesus obviously was the superior. He was showing that HIS Kingdom is the ultimate power since He was able to override the authority of the reigning principalities in the given territory. I believe what Jesus was actually saying in verse 29 was, "For what kingdom is powerful enough to enter the devil's kingdom (where Satan has legal, acquired ground) and override his authority? Only a kingdom that is stronger - a kingdom that could neutralize the devil's authority and plunder his property."

In as much as the strongest Kingdom could take over all of the earth, however, the Kingdom of God did set parameters into place whereby even the Kingdom of God is subject. The earth is God's according to Psalm 24 but God did give man dominion over it. So, ultimately, it is always up to man to determine which of the two supernatural kingdoms would reign over his personal life and space. This is evident in the fact that Jesus only exercised His divine authority of the Kingdom of God where it was sought, chosen, welcomed or invited by the people. He never overrode a man's will with His. He never used Kingdom of God authority to help people who didn't want it. He gave man the right to choose if they wanted to continue in their slavery to the present ruling power they were comfortable and familiar with - or reject it for the new, far superior authority that had come upon them through Christ which offered so many benefits.

As the years passed and I became more familiar with the Word of God, I began to understand more deeply that in the Kingdom of God system, all things are infinite and supernatural. And if we enter into that system while on earth, it would radically alter our natural lives as we know them! I deduced that the more I walk "in" the divine system of God, the more my life will manifest its reality as opposed to the limited nature of the realm I physically reside in. I also understood that our "if we do this" mentality (like give, for example) then "God will do that" isn't fully accurate. It is now my contention that when "we do this" (give) then we are operating according to the Kingdom of God government so the "God will do that" part is not God doing anything more. He already did it all and the "that" is manifest through our obedience - or alignment with it.

For another example, dwelling in the secret place and hiding in the shadow of the Almighty doesn't compel God to protect someone, rather, it's automatic when practicing Kingdom of God principles. Because by hiding in Him, we have entered into Kingdom of God dynamics wherein divine protection lies. Likewise, seeking first the Kingdom of God and His righteousness automatically sets into motion that all the desires of our hearts shall be added unto us. By applying the Kingdom of God principle of seeking God first, we 'inherit' the Kingdom of God dynamics wherein all our desires are manifest. And what about thanksgiving to God or forgiveness of others or giving generously? These are Kingdom of God principles and when they are practiced on earth, the dynamics of the realm of the Kingdom of God are made manifest and we inherit those supernatural, Holy Kingdom benefits.

The Bible is loaded with what will happen if a Kingdom of God statute is put into effect or followed… operated in… or 'entered into'. We must understand that the Kingdom of God is about principles pertaining to believing and trusting God, to loving even the unlovable, being selfless, and being of pure, righteous ambition. This is demonstrated in Romans 14:17, "For the kingdom of God is not a matter of eating and drinking, but of

righteousness, peace and joy in the Holy Spirit..." This is why God avails His Kingdom to us while we are still here. The fall of man brought such defeat and loss to our realm. The Lord simply made a way that glory and His goodness, which entails full victory, can manifest amongst us yet again. But we have to go after it and come into it proactively. It doesn't just happen by believing Christ died our death only. It happens by also
agreeing with everything else He said and living it! The devil doesn't give up trying to dominate our lives just because we become born of Spirit. Not in the least. That's when it's time for him to keep us from discovering the all and all of Christ!

    As much as the Bible demonstrates how we can bring God's Kingdom to life in our world, it is equally descriptive about what will happen if a believer walks outside of Kingdom of God statutes. The following passage declares that willfully doing wrong keeps one from receiving the benefits of the Kingdom of God! In 1 Corinthians 6:6-20 Paul is addressing CHRISTIANS, not the unsaved. I point this out to illustrate that it's after somebody is saved and is a "believer" where our actions are what determine our ability to benefit from the extraordinary, supernatural blessings afforded us by the Kingdom of God which, as Jesus said, is "at hand".

    1 Corinthians 6:6-20 NIV, "But instead, one brother takes another to court—and this in front of unbelievers! The very fact that you have lawsuits among you means you have been completely defeated already. Why not rather be wronged? Why not rather be cheated? Instead, you yourselves cheat and do wrong, and you do this to your brothers and sisters. Or do you not know that wrongdoers will not inherit the kingdom of God? Do not be deceived: Neither the sexually immoral nor idolaters nor adulterers nor men who have sex with men nor thieves nor the greedy nor drunkards nor slanderers nor swindlers will inherit the

kingdom of God. And that is what some of you were. But you were washed, you were sanctified, you were justified in the name of the Lord Jesus Christ and by the Spirit of our God".

Whether or not somebody can "lose" their salvation by willfully practicing sin is a whole other topic of discussion. My point with this passage is simply that Paul is urging believers to see that choosing to live a lifestyle that is not in agreement with the Kingdom of God keeps them from experiencing the Kingdom of God and ultimately, the fullness of Christ.

Let's bring this home... Within the Kingdom of God lies all that God offers which is fullness of joy, no sorrow, perfect peace, and pure, unending love. In Heaven there is abundance, supernatural multiplication, divine wisdom, unending resources, grand revelation and knowing. In Heaven everything is whole and perfect. There is no sickness or disease. Therefore, I believe the more we who have been born of Spirit walk in and operate according to Heavenly principles, the more we know the entirety of that which Is Written, apply it, profess it, and stand on it no matter what the natural kingdom OR the dark kingdom is suggesting, the more we unleash the Kingdom of God and all its supernatural benefits. And the more we activate the Kingdom of God in this world.

Again, the Kingdom of God isn't "Heaven" but it is the divine system of Heaven which a believer can partake of while still on earth. The Kingdom of God which is glory, wonder, and might... is at hand indeed! When we abide in Christ, which is to love Him with our whole hearts, obey His Word and follow His ways, we are privy to His divine system. What is most interesting, though, is unlike every other kingdom where there are sanctions implemented within those kingdoms when regulations are not practiced, the Kingdom of God has no sanctioning process within it! Rather, you just don't get to experience and partake of it if you don't walk within its parameters! In fact, the only way you CAN inherit the dynamics of the realm of the Kingdom of God is by receiving Jesus as Savior and then truly and adamantly seeking His Kingdom and His righteousness above all else! We can say then, essentially, that putting on Christ's sandals and being like Him is how we step into the realm called the Kingdom of God. And there's no other place we should rather be.

Things To Consider

How much would you rather walk in the divine dynamics of the Kingdom of God?

Chapter Review Checkpoints

1. There are many earthly, natural kingdoms but there are only TWO supernatural kingdoms. Those two kingdoms are: _____ and _____ _____.

2. The natural kingdom of earth and all of its dynamics includes decay and deterioration. The supernatural kingdom of darkness dynamics include death, loss, and destruction. But fortunately, the Kingdom of God dynamics include:

A. fullness of joy, perfect peace, restoration and unending love

B. supernatural multiplication, divine intervention and abundance,

C. divine revelation, miracles, power to overcome sin and the devil

D. all of the above

3. The "Kingdom of God" is another term for

A. Heaven

B. Heaven's government and dynamics

4. God's promises instantly manifest in our lives upon our redemption. We don't need to do anything but sit back and be thankful Christ died our death.

T or F

5. If you "inherit the Kingdom", this means

A. Kingdom of God dynamics are manifest in your life on earth and you benefit from them

B. you will go to Heaven when you die

6. We cannot and will not inherit Kingdom of God and its benefits if we willfully live a lifestyle of sin.

T or F

7. Knowing what the Bible says is not enough. In order for the Life of the Word to be loosed to reign over us, we MUST:

    A. share it with others

    B. believe it, apply it, profess it, and stand on it no matter what

    C. be able to recite it word for word

    D. quickly reference it in any given situation where it applies

8. When we abide in Christ by loving Him with our whole hearts and obey His ways, the Holy Kingdom benefits manifest in our lives.

T or F

ANSWER KEY - CHAPTER IV
1-God's Kingdom, Satan's kingdom, 2-D, 3-B, 4-F, 5-A, 6-T, 7-B, 8-T

Chapter Five
The Rise Of The False Prophet

Revelations 16:13 NIV says, "Then I saw three impure spirits that looked like frogs; they came out of the mouth of the dragon, out of the mouth of the beast and out of the mouth of the false prophet."

If we study Revelations 12 and 13, by the time we get to the above passage, we can deduce that these three entities constitute the evil trinity. Just as we who follow Christ believe in the Holy Trinity - Father, Son (Jesus Christ) and Holy Spirit, I believe Revelations 16:13 establishes that the devil, too, set himself up as an entity with three distinct parts. The dragon is the father, or Satan. The "son" is the spirit of antichrist. And the counterfeit of the Holy Spirit is the false prophet. We can deduce this because of the roles these different beasts play in these passages.

Please review the chart on the following page which lays out how the devil mimics God in his mission to become god.

Satan

Goal: Become god over all the earth
Strategy: Infiltrate and corrupt earth's two base life systems
Government & Religion
To accomplish this, Satan mimics the triune entity of the Almighty God by appointing two beasts into positions that counterfeit Jesus Christ and the Holy Spirit.

Jesus Christ's Counterfeit is the **Antichrist** (Revelations 12, 13 and 16:13)	**The Holy Spirit's Counterfeit** is the **False Prophet** (Revelations 13:11-15 and 16:13)
Just as Jesus came to establish the way, the truth, and the government of God, the spirit of Antichrist is here to establish the false government which functions completely contrary to Christ's. The spirit of Antichrist must destroy liberty and take over every nation's system of government from the bottom up; completely eliminating every shred of right government.	Just as the Holy Spirit came to point the way to Christ and empower believers with supernatural gifts like tongues, knowledge, and miracles, the false prophet does the same through numerous demons (since he is not omnipresent) but promotes his evil kingdom. The false prophet's mission is to destroy the Gospel of Christ and infiltrate the world with false religion, idolatrly, and corrupt spirituality. And he must destroy, constrict, or confound everyone who gets in his way.

Briefly, the spirit of antichrist's agenda is to corrupt governmental, political and economic systems. This operation is the first system Satan set into place to accomplish his mission to become a literal god over all the earth. He's been working on this for thousands of years and we can see that he's come a long way. The spirit of antichrist is soon to make his debut in the form of a man and become the god of the earth. However, I will not be spending any time elaborating on this particular operation but understand that this is the role the spirit of antichrist plays in Satan's endeavors to become the god of our world. Because while Jesus came to present the Kingdom of God's government and its benefits, its liberty and power, the spirit of antichrist is here to infiltrate the world's natural governments and set up his false systems within them.

Then, as the chart illustrates, just as the Holy Spirit was sent to empower us, give us revelation, guide and comfort us, teach us, impart spiritual gifts to us as He chooses, etc., the COUNTERFEIT holy spirit operates in the same fashion but for the sake of dismantling the reality and power of the one TRUE God and promoting the devil who aspires to literally BECOME god. Just as the Holy Spirit gives utterance (tongues/prophetic words), Holy revelation, divine insight and understanding, the false prophet likewise gives utterance or psychic revelation, demonic insight and corrupt knowledge. The Holy Spirit was sent to unveil the truth of God's Word, Who bears witness to the Gospel of Christ, Who leads us and guides us in all spiritual truths. The false prophet is the counterfeit who creates false religions, cults, and depraved spiritualism. He influxes those who are spiritually intuitive (who are likewise blind) with depraved cultic notions. He goes after those who are not grounded in truth and are gullible to receive whatever supernatural malarkey he dishes out. He provides supernatural helps and answers the misguided world is seeking - only they are his evil delusions, not God's truth. And his two-fold operation is to first replace the Gospel of Christ with false religions, and second, to hinder, suffocate, or dominate believers who are a potential threat to his agenda. And the bigger the threat one is, the more avidly he works to keep them from realizing truth. Ultimately, he knows he must keep us as distant from God as possible so that we don't become a hindrance to his dark kingdom!

While the operations at work in the political and economical arena are equally significant, the purpose of this title is to expose the false prophet because he's the one who is behind the destruction of the church and the promoting of the spirit of python's empire. He's the master who orchestrated this particular operation. Watch as it unfolds...

God addresses false prophets all through scripture (Isaiah 44:25, Jeremiah 14:14, Jeremiah 23:16, Lamentations 2:14), to name a few. Let's look closely at Ezekiel 13:9 NIV which reads, *"My hand will be against the prophets who see false visions and utter lying divinations."* What this tells us is that false prophets are not prophets of God who make mistakes in what they believe God spoke to them, rather, they are prophets who are getting their information from the false kingdom; from THE false prophet, from the counterfeit holy spirit himself and these are the prophets God is passionately against. Because if they aren't getting their "divine" input from God, then they're getting it from Satan's kingdom and this is detestable. Keep this in mind and watch as I lay out the framework of what became a demonic empire through which millions of people would be ruled - saved or otherwise.

We have taken a step back and considered Satan's primary mission, which is to rule over all the earth via his vast and ever growing kingdom, so now we can better appreciate his logic in setting up specific platforms through which to achieve his ends - such as the false prophet's empire which I refer to as Operation Python. Through this extraordinary dynasty, Satan works diligently to keep God's church under foot. The devil, in order to be god, had to keep mankind separated from the real God, true religion, and the power of God. So, the false prophet, thereby, would have to create false religions and cults, set up wrong systems of belief and practices in civilizations as a whole, as well as infiltrate the true church by ruling subtly over the children of the Mighty God. By dominating all aspects of 'religion', the divine, or what man believes, Satan would rule as god. So, this is what defines the false prophet's agenda from ancient times to this present hour.

Clearly, the devil could accomplish ruling man through many means but idolatry happened to fuel the most prominent liaisons between Satan and man. What the false prophet did was played on mankind's fascination and need to connect with the mysterious powers of the supernatural. The devil knew that man sensed there was something mighty in the unseen realm whereby we could get information on how to run our lives or simply find healing for our bodies, for example, if we connected to it. Satan knew that humans were desperate for divine revelation and divination birthed out of idolatry (the worship of false gods) would be his tool. And it worked so effectively. Ancient civilizations everywhere had false gods set into place and practiced divination. It was popular and quite the norm. It was even practiced as part of their religions! They all created the false gods and then cried out to the invisible realm for answers. And they got them. This is worse than any movie ever made depicting the rise of an evil power over a people who fell for its tricks.

Acts 16:16-18 KJV says, *"And it came to pass, as we went to prayer, a certain damsel possessed with a spirit of divination met us, which brought her masters much gain by soothsaying: The same followed Paul and us, and cried, saying, These men are the servants of the most high God, which shew unto us the way of salvation. And this did she many days. But Paul, being grieved, turned and said to the spirit, I command thee in the name of Jesus Christ to come out of her. And he came out the same hour."*

The Greek term used in verse sixteen for divination is pythos, or python. But why is this? What does a snake have to do with a woman who is given utterance by a demonic spirit?

I'm no scholar of ancient history or mythology but find what I've learned to be quite fascinating when realizing the impact it has had on our world through the ages. As I said, divination laid the foundation through which Satan, through the counterfeit holy spirit, would gain tremendous ground over the spiritual aspects of mankind.

Divination is the art of seeking answers, guidance, or revelation through supernatural means. It was first known to have been practiced by a people called the Sumerians. According to Sumerian myth, humans were created to serve their gods. But how were they to know what the gods expected or wanted from them? This necessitated the arts of divination which, through various means, mankind could communicate with their gods. How perfect is that? Satan could certainly accommodate! And that's where the false prophet came in…

Since subsequent civilizations followed the same notion of needing gods to turn to for protection, they, too, incorporated the art and developed practices whereby their gods could reveal their demands or guidance. Though each culture had their own form of idolatry saturating their lives and developed their own techniques of deciphering what their gods (the false prophet) were saying, divination was widely practiced everywhere, and the false prophet suddenly had huge shoes to fill.

The people of ancient Italy, the Etruscians, practiced Alectryomancy which is where the diviner observes birds. Psychics would draw a circle with the letters of their alphabet on the ground and put grain next to each letter. Then they'd ask a question and let a rooster or hen loose to eat the grain. The letter would be written down when the bird ate its grain and the diviner would hopefully acquire a sensible answer - much like the Ouija board does in our culture today. The primary difference in usage in American culture, however, is users are sometimes only seeking personal enlightenment whereas ancient civilizations relied on such guidance for the leading of their people.

Alectryomancy (or currently, Zoomancy) is still used even today. The Zande tribe of Africa rely on ants to determine what their gods want by placing two leaves on an ant hill. An ant eating the left leaf means 'yes' while eating the right leaf means 'no'.

Dare I say it? Despite being the most civilized culture of all times, we Americans also practice Alectryomancy. What? How? No way! We don't rely on creatures to determine what's going to happen! Ahh, but we do. Every February 2nd some of us observe whether or not the groundhog will see his shadow which will determine the length of winter. See how sneaky!

There were other 'mancies' concerning the usage of animals in determining what the gods were saying - such as Felidomancy (cats), Hippomanic (horses), Ichthyomancy (fish) and Ornthomancy (flight of birds). But one of the more popular 'mancies' observed by many civilizations was Ophimancy which was the observance of the behavior of snakes. Hmmm....

Amazingly, seeking guidance through animals is only one divinatory technique. There are countless others. Divination is any practice which utilizes the observance of something natural to decipher what the supernatural realm is "revealing". And again, it's for the sake of tapping into the powers that be, their named gods (or the false prophet), for guidance.

Understand that regardless of the medium selected or the civilization and system of gods established, people didn't presume the rooster, pebble, or snake was the power. Rather, these were the tools they consecrated to their gods to speak to and guide them through. But who really were these powers that be? If these gods were made up, how could they provide answers through a hen eating grain or an ant eating a leaf?

It needs to be appreciated that even though their gods were not real, the false prophet gave the created gods "life" which made their gods a reality. Today we may call the belief in their gods mythology, but it was very real in their eyes and hearts. And there is always power in what we believe.

So, naturally the devil, after observing a particular civilization's style and longings, worked willfully with the zealots of each culture to establish false gods that met their personal fancies but through which he himself could manifest and rule. Satan knew his power relied upon mankind creating him a platform, a medium, through which his supernatural kingdom could manifest in the natural realm where man was granted dominion. He knew he could rule anywhere man gave him a place to rule. Hence, every god mankind created was a medium for the devil. Consider how beneficial it was that they even named the gods according to a specific attribute, strength, or nature whereby a specific, relative spirit of darkness could assume the role. It's absolutely phenomenal. Satan had found a vice in mankind where, all through history, every class of people would 'need' to implement some sort of system of beliefs which would connect them to the supernatural - and he would always be sure to accommodate. Anything to reduce God to nothing and exult himself to ill-conceived glory.

Isn't it interesting how it wasn't even that a bare minimum of gods were created? How it was, rather, that god after god after god throughout nation after nation was created? After so many of them came into 'being' and even crossed over into other cultures, I wonder how it was possible for anyone to know which god was the right one! (But of course, I'm coming from the perspective that there is only one God.)

Have you ever heard of the term oracle? If not, it's a person, most often a woman, through whom a god is believed to speak. It could also be a shrine dedicated as the place where a deity reveals hidden knowledge, guidance, or divine purpose through such a person.

So far we've discussed how, through idolatry, the false prophet used divination as a medium through which to 'be god' but the day did come whereby people, mainly women or sacred shrines, more prominently became those mediums. Today we are likely to refer to such mediums as psychics. But in ancient times they were oracles and were very sacred culturally. In fact, there was a particular oracle site in Ancient Greece that became "the" oracle of all oracles and is, I believe, what instituted the vast, dark empire I call Operation Python.

In doing the research for this topic I found it to be challenging to distinguish actual events from the myths because Greek mythology is presented as though it were reality. For example, there really was a place called Delphi in Greece. There really was a site at Delphi where a shrine was set up that became an extremely famous oracle for seeking answers from the gods. Yet, the origin and some of the history of the oracle are mythological.

Such as Gaea, the mythological entity known as mother earth who was the main goddess over all the Greek gods (who, interestingly enough, later married her son, the sky, whom she'd single handedly created) and to whom the Oracle of Delphi belonged. These were the gods worshiped prior to the Hellenes (Greeks) introducing the cult of Zeus, from what I understand. Anyway, the Encyclopedia Britannica 2010 - Encyclopedia Britannica Online states, "According to legend, the oracle at Delphi originally belonged to Gaea, the Earth goddess, and was guarded by her child Python, the serpent." ~ Python?

Under the reference for python, the Encyclopedia Britannica 2010 states, "Python, in Greek mythology, a huge serpent that was killed by the god Apollo at Delphi either because it would not let him found his oracle, being accustomed itself to giving oracles, or because it had persecuted Apollo's mother, Leto, during her pregnancy. In the earliest account, the Homeric Hymn to Apollo, the serpent is nameless and female, but later it is male, as in Euripides' Iphigenia Among the Taurians, and named Python (found first in the account of the 4th-century-bc historian Ephorus; Pytho was the old name for Delphi)."

From Secret Teachings of all Ages: Wonders of Antiquity by Manly P. Hall; 1928 - [Copyright not renewed] at http://www.sacred-texts.com/eso/sta/sta14.htm :

"The oracle of Apollo at Delphi remains one of the unsolved mysteries of the ancients. Alexander Wilder derives the name Delphi from delphos, the womb. This name was chosen by the Greeks because of the shape of the cavern and the vent leading into the depths of the earth. The original name of the oracle was Pytho, so called because its chambers had been the abode of the great serpent Python, a fearsome creature that had crept out of the slime left by the receding flood that had destroyed all human beings except Deucalion and Pyrrha. Apollo, climbing the side of Mount Parnassus, slew the serpent after a prolonged combat, and threw the body down the fissure of the oracle. From that time the Sun God, surnamed the Pythian Apollo, gave oracles from the vent. With Dionysos he shared the honor of being the patron god of Delphi.

After being vanquished by Apollo, the spirit of Python (the false prophet?) remained at Delphi as the representative of his conqueror, and it was with the aid of his effluvium that the priestess was able to become en rapport with the god. The fumes rising from the fissure of the oracle were supposed to come from the decaying body of Python. The name Pythoness, or Pythia, given to the female hierophant of the oracle, means literally one who has been thrown into a religious frenzy by inhaling fumes rising from decomposing matter. It is of further interest to note that the Greeks believed the oracle of Delphi to be the umbilicus of the earth, thus proving that they considered the planet an immense human being. The connection between the principle of oracular revelation and the occult significance of the navel is an important secret belonging to the ancient Mysteries.

The oracle, however, is much older than the foregoing account indicates. A story of this kind was probably invented by the priests to explain the phenomena to those inquisitive persons whom they did not consider worthy of enlightenment regarding the true esoteric nature of the oracle. Some believe that the Delphic fissure was discovered by a Hypoborean priest, but as far back as recorded history goes the cave was sacred, and persons came from all parts of Greece and the surrounding countries to question the demon who dwelt in its chimney-like vent. Priests and priestesses guarded it closely and served the spirit who dwelt therein and who enlightened humanity through the gift of prophecy."

Are you seeing what I am seeing? The devil, more specifically, the counterfeit holy spirit (or false prophet) established himself as a divine guide like the real Holy Spirit is to believers - only he did it through the fame of a snake shrine. And because this particular oracle soared unlike any other divinatory shrine, the spirit of python (which was endowed by the false prophet) became infamous in Greece and abroad.

Based on my findings from Wikipedia, the free encyclopedia, under the listing for Delphi, countless artifacts were found at the settlement site such as pottery, bronze works, as well as tripod dedications. Apparently these streamed in more steadily than those contributed to Olympia. Neither the range of objects nor the prestigious dedications proves that Delphi was a point of focus for numerous worshipers but the amount of high value goods found there and in no other sanctuary suggests it was. It is believed the Oracle's influence spanned through all the Greek world and was consulted before wars, the founding of colonies, and when other such guidance was required. The claim is that even the semi-Hellenic countries such as Lydia, Caria, and Egypt respected the Oracle.

We can see how the soaring success of the Delphi Oracle became a grand platform for the devil and his appointed, counterfeit holy spirit. Satan had discovered a huge fault in the hearts of man that he could monopolize if he were diligent and strategic! He knew that every nation longed for a god or gods to worship, serve, and be guided by. Idolatry was his ticket to success. So he sent the false prophet on a mission to manifest through these idols and more specifically, a snake shrine, to aid these ancient cultures.

It is my contention that the false prophet saw to it he gave forth the most amazing revelations he possibly could and impressed everyone who came to the oracle of Delphi for help. He seized the opportunity to convince them of his manifest presence and power. He showed himself strong and touched the hearts and lives of people by the hundreds and even thousands. And they paid homage to the Oracle by bringing gifts to the site. The more they brought offerings, the greater he manifested through the oracles or priestesses. The false prophet gleaned such power via this worship and faith in his works that it established him a name in the natural realm for millennia to come. And the name? Python.

Things To Consider
Would the "spirit of python" be known or exist today had there never been a false prophet who brought the Python such notoriety in ancient Greece?

Chapter Review Checkpoints

1. The devil counterfeits everything the Lord God does. Since our God is a triune entity, Father, Son, and Holy Spirit, the devil also has three parts. Name them:

The evil father is known as _____.
The evil son of the devil is the spirit of _____.
The devil's counterfeit for the Holy Spirit is the _____.

2. The counterfeit holy spirit, who the scriptures call the 2nd beast or the false prophet, is the evil entity behind everything that happens which pertains to false prophetic utterance, the worship of false gods, evil signs and wonders such as occurs in sorcery or voodoo, etc. But in the way the Holy Spirit does everything to promote the Gospel of Christ, the false prophet only tries to indoctrinate unbelievers with false spirituality or religion. He leaves Christians alone because it is too late to corrupt them or come between them and their God.
T or F

3. Satan set up a platform through the worship of false gods and divination whereby the false prophet could spiritually infiltrate our lives and rule. Because of the Oracle of Delphi where a snake was endowed with supernatural

power, the name this platform and operation took on was called _____.

4. According to the revelation the Holy Spirit gave Paula, the spirit of python is actually an 'operation' or a vast system of powers and principalities of darkness under the leadership of the false prophet who work together to accomplish a unified agenda which is to bring Satan to full power over the earth.

T of F

5. The only way the spirit of python can gain legal access into our lives is if we practice the art of divination.

T or F

6. Divination was instituted by the devil and anything the devil institutes, he rules over. So, if you agree with the idea that even playfully relying on an a "Magic 8 Ball" for answers is okay to do, you are stepping into kingdom of darkness territory and are subjecting yourself to the devil's authority.

T or F

7. We exalt and magnify the devil every time we participate in anything that he instituted in our world and this gives him legal authority over us.

T or F

8. If we rely on things like material things, status, or money, to the point where they are what our hope is in and what makes us happy, then these are false sources which are likewise, false gods.

T or F

ANSWER KEY - CHAPTER V
1-Satan, Antichrist, False Prophet; 2-F, 3-Python, 4-T, 5-F, 6-T, 7-T, 8-T

Chapter Six
It's Just A Namesake

I believe that when Paul cast the spirit of python out of the woman, he went after the kingpin. Paul addressed the big dog that was behind the ridiculous charade...

"*Oh, **people**, puh-**lease hear** me* when I say that these ***marvelous** **men** **surely*** are servants of the Most High God who show us the way unto salvation!"

Because the woman was using her demonically inspired gift of prophetic utterance to draw attention to herself as well as gain the favor of genuine men of God, it has been concluded that these are the primary nature or behavioral manifestations of the python spirit - to be an attention getter, use extreme flattery, and to have the ability to prophesy via demonic aid. But the Holy Spirit is the author of divine utterance yet this is not the only supernatural way He manifests His power. I contend, therefore, that it is the same for the counterfeit in that he does so much more than the behaviors the damsel depicted.

As we discussed, the false prophet mimics the attributes of the Holy Spirit but he must set himself up in our world via idolatry and then guides us into false beliefs, false practices, and sin, comforts us through false dependencies or resources, inspires false faith-based ideologies which are contrary to truth and the Gospel of Christ, empowers people demonically, speaks through voices 'prophetically', and speaks to man through visions (hallucinations) and dreams. Just as the Holy Spirit is the believer's teacher and unveils the mysteries of the scriptures, the counterfeit works to conceal the mysteries of scripture and even distort them. Just as the Holy Spirit moves on man supernaturally to empower him to higher places in God, the counterfeit moves on man to deplete him, squash him, and separate him from God. It's simple. Everything the Holy Spirit does, the false prophet does the opposite in attempt to squeeze the breath of life out of us. ~The Holy Spirit breathes life into man, the false prophet sucks it out. Now isn't that what the python does?

We've also discussed how the false prophet rose to power and position because of the grand platform the Oracle at Delphi and other mediums provided him. We established that a mythological snake was merely the medium the counterfeit holy spirit used to speak to man through. These were the tools through which the false prophet made his 'manifest presence' known. The false prophet and his system of demons were the power source that made the Oracle of Delphi python terribly huge. In fact, the false prophet made the python so grand that it took on its own identity. And because this identity was so profound, it carried itself down through the ages.

Or was it, in fact, the python snake that was its own power source? Or perhaps just a bunch of random, fantastic uttering demons with no agenda should be credited for the amazing power the oracle exuded? I don't think so. I believe these workers had a purpose and I'm convinced it was to give the false prophet a platform so that he would be known and venerated through the ages - so that his empire could more effectively squash truth and infuse falsities.

So, you see… just because he used the woman in Acts 16 according to the snake's infamous reputation didn't mean that's all there was to the spirit who possessed her. The false prophet who dominated the damsel had big time plans in the works against the Apostle Paul. His intention was to do so much more than just utter or flatter. His goal was to shut Paul and his partners down.

That's why I insist that this python spirit is merely another name the counterfeit holy spirit came to go by. And because it's the false prophet's job to set up false ways and dismantle holy ones, he will employ countless types of demons, powers and principalities to do his bidding!

Unfortunately, we cannot sort out all of the identities of the dark kingdom workers. But let's consider the teachings of two of the most popularly named spirits: the Jezebel spirit and the spirit of witchcraft. When we look at how they operate and their behavioral manifestations, we see many parallels. They both promote extreme sensuality. They both use sex. They both utilize manipulation and control. They both involve pride and being the one in command over the Godly. Yet, they've each acquired their own, separate names. But if we look at what each of their final goals are, suddenly, they are both in the exact same boat serving the exact same purpose - which ultimately is to do what? To dismantle God's truths or take over his church. To be the reigning force. Regardless of the spirit at work, Satan is the one exulted and the truth of Jesus Christ is squashed....or 'constricted'.

After looking at it like this, we can see that it could also have been the spirit of Jezebel that was operating through the woman who followed Paul so faithfully. Perhaps she was trying to seduce Paul into her favor? Who knows. All I am saying is that the evil motives and driving force behind her declarations that the men were servants of the Most High God, were above all else, a service to Satan by the power and inspiration of the false prophet and his need to put an end to the Apostle Paul's influential ministry.

Just think about it. Paul was a powerful man of God so we know Satan was on to him! There is no doubt the devil was desperate to find a way to bring Paul down so that he would stop bringing people out of deception and into truth. Paul's teachings were doing more than introducing the Light of the world. They were dismantling all the idolatry in the nations the false prophet had strategically set into place throughout the previous centuries. Paul was in direct opposition to the false prophet! He was messing everything up! He was undoing all the false prophet's work. Clearly, Paul needed addressed and the false prophet would personally go after him. So, he caressed Paul with the praise and affirmation so that he could hopefully become entwined with or embraced by Paul. So that he could lure Paul into darkness and ultimately, defeat. Maybe the false prophet wanted to use the girl to lure him into a sexual snare or even a conversation where he, being bewitched by her beauty, perhaps, might agree with some false thing she'd suggest. Something... ANYTHING. Anything that could give the devil legal grounds to move in and hinder the power of God.

Fortunately, Paul was so close to the Lord, grounded in truth and filled with the glorious Holy Spirit that he saw right through the woman the false prophet was using. And Paul cast him out. Had Paul not done this, I believe the counterfeit holy spirit would have done major damage to Paul's ministry and the Bible would not be as we know it is today. But Paul put him out, praise God.

Presuming that the spirit of python's behavioral manifestations are strictly indicative of the specific nature of the woman's actions in Acts 16 is not looking at the whole picture. The fact is there are countless 'false prophet' type spirits. Jezebel herself was considered a seductive false prophet (Revelations 2:20). Like I said, the woman following Paul could easily be accused of having the spirit of Jezebel! Perhaps she was buttering them up and demonstrating her high quality prophetic insight so that maybe they'd add her to their team and use her? Only for her to subtly bring idolatry to the table or perhaps, take over and become the controlling power??

This is all speculation but shows that this woman's behavior should not become the explicit, definitive description of how the spirit of python works. It's only a small part of a vast picture. Because when we look at who this python spirit really is and then consider his overall agenda, we cannot determine to limit his nature to the acts portrayed in one single woman.

The reason I feel it's important to grasp this is because we tend to spend so much time deciphering the ways various spirits move amongst us - especially through churches - putting our emphasis on what spirit is behind the different attacks. That it's a spirit of Jezebel if the person does x, but a spirit of witchcraft if a the person does y. When ultimately, regardless of the tactic, regardless of which spirit does what, the end result is to suck the life out of the church. (Isn't this the false prophet's job? To rid the earth of true faith so he can one day point the way to the Antichrist? And if he is going to succeed at this, does he not have the terrific burden of bringing the bride to impotency? Is this not what the python does to its prey?) At any rate, I believe we need to spend less time deciphering the traits of the spirits, worrying about who did what, and just do what Paul did by going straight for the jugular.

As the story goes, the damsel's owners found out she wouldn't be making them any more money so they seized Paul and Silas, put them before the magistrates, and had them thrown into prison. This passage reveals how intolerant the spirit of python is to being opposed. Imagine the false prophet's rage when, instead of Paul being seduced by the spirit and his ministry muted, he recognized the false prophet's presence and cast him out! What a shock this must have been to the empire which was accustomed to victory! What fury this must have wrought. I can almost hear the arrogance of the false prophet sneering at Paul saying, "What? You think you can waltz into my territory, undo my work, and then cast ME out and get away with it???"

We know the men who lost business were ticked, but I'm confident that a spirit of python minion spoke rage into their ears demanding justice and then screamed into the magistrate's, "Go ahead, throw them into prison! Show them they can't come here and interfere with our lives! Make them an example!" The python stopped at nothing to see Paul and Silas locked up and torn down to size. He would squash them and make them want to think twice about being so faithful to their cause; to their Jesus. He'd make them regret standing up for the Christ and daring to assault his idolatrous systems. He figured he'd beat them down and mess them over so hard that they'd shrink and, upon eventual release from prison, would go away quietly with their tails between their legs.

On the contrary, we know the end of the story how through Paul and Silas's praise and worship the power of GOD showed up and the significantly lesser rule of python was dramatically overturned! Hallelujah!

All this to show... The spirit of python was more than "a" demon spirit. He was the false prophet who ruled an empire of spirits through which he tirelessly works at pulling people away from the light and into idolatry and false spirituality. Who works all the harder at squashing anyone who opposes his work. And within that empire, demons such as the spirit of Jezebel, witchcraft, isolation, oppression, and even infirmity (to name a few), are strategically employed.

The irony, I believe, is we've perceived that the spirit of python is a power equal to or compatible with the spirit of Jezebel. As though they are two different reigning powers who have their own separate agendas. But I believe the spirit of Jezebel is merely one of the spirits working within Operation Python's (or the false prophet's) system.

Consider this hypothetical scenario... You have a church where there's a great deal of strife and dissension that's been escalating, a split appears eminent and the discernment is that a spirit of Jezebel is the cause. However, the truth is that the spirit of Jezebel is but one force at work in that situation. The Jezebel spirit may be the one going after the pastor, but there have to be other demons coordinating and manipulating and working in conjunction with her in order that she accomplishes her goal. The spirits all work together. And it's not that the false prophet has "teamed up" with her by coming in by her side to constrict certain members or speak false utterance from them only, rather, the false prophet is the ruling spirit who has been running the entire operation. Remember, it is the false prophet's agenda to bring his father, Satan, into power as god. It's their mission to take over and stifle God's people; the church. Jezebel shares in this goal despite the fact that her specialty is to dominate powerful leaders. That's her singular task amidst the entire operation of the devil's ploy to take over the church. Meanwhile, the spirit of python's tactics are broad. And he's the one who sets all the forces like Jezebel into place and strategizes the attack which, if all the demons accomplish their individual tasks, the entire body of believers goes under. Do this worldwide… throughout the entire body of Christ and Satan will have it made. I mean, think about it. The spirit of Jezebel, while specifically in charge of ruling a church body via its head (pastor) is but ONE means to the ultimate endeavor of destroying God's body. She doesn't have her own, separate agenda. Her agenda is OF the python's agenda.

Now, if my suggestion that the python spirit is, in fact, the false prophet is still too difficult to digest, try to look at it from the following perspective:

If we were to take the time to analyze every single act of any power or principality of darkness, do you suppose we could connect them to either the spirit of antichrist or the false prophet? Let's hypothetically presume that the demonic worker asserting strategy against things having to do with government or the economy - anything having to do with the influx of rules &

regulations, or the infringement on rights and freedoms, is overseen by the spirit of antichrist. Likewise, let's say the demonic worker asserting strategy against things connected to spirituality, religion, or faith - anything having to do with dismantling God's gospel and promoting any number of corrupt, decrepit systems of false belief, is overseen by the false prophet. If this were indeed the case, I wonder if every single plot is intended to promote either of these two systems in the world, bar none. From people's selfishness to personal addictions to spousal conflict to large scale crime and even abortion.

If this were the case and you wanted to go after these two primary systems in our world, government and religion, where would you start? It wouldn't take rocket science to figure out that you would begin with the family unit. What you would ultimately need to do is corrupt and divide everything from the bottom up. Division equals strife and disorder. So, first, put family members against each other, especially spouses. If you can split them up via strife, being a demonic force, you not only now have your claws dug deeper into them and can probably tempt them into darker areas of sin and bondage, but you also have children who've witnessed poor behavior whose lives will be altered and not positively or healthily influenced (and I'm not even touching on the spiritual aspects!). The kids are likely to have emotional or behavioral problems in their development and they'll likely be even less stable as adults than mom and dad were; even more controlled by sin and evil. In the meantime, you keep pushing for division. Promote stress, cause disorder and chaos in all the littlest ways you can in all the corners of the world. Program everyone to be unstable and desperate for resolve but incapable of finding it because they are too self-seeking and morally bankrupt.

If you strategize it right, and you also manage to infiltrate the media and government and all the infrastructures that make this world go 'round, you can play everybody against each other and, within mere decades, bring entire nations to chaos.

We think our nations are declining because we've put the wrong people into office but the truth is, and we all know it because we're always talking about it, the decline started in the home. But is this because the people of recent times suddenly decided to not care about keeping the family unit intact and healthy? No. What we have done is lost touch with truth, God, and have given ourselves over to the flesh, idolatry and in some cases, every form of evil. The devil has weaseled his way into the family and we've permitted it by our negligence and ignorance. And the end result is the nations are headed for certain chaos which will conveniently require a demonically infiltrated system of government to assume the role as savior and provider of resolve.

Since Satan's goal is to literally become god, he's had organized forces in place working very strategically to do anything and everything to dismantle everything that is right and good in our world! So you see, the young girl having the abortion or the teen who is already sucked into addiction, or the old woman who cannot forgive her pastor, or the wife who is leaving her husband for no good reason… these may all be personal issues but tie them all together and what do you have but division, strife, disorder, and eventually, chaos. Duplicate this to the masses once you've got your foot in every infrastructure, create the perfect plot to lure the disorderly nation to national upheaval and eventually you have a nation that's upside down, destroying each other, and completely gullible for a lying antichrist who will present a very delusional but attractive solution.

The reason I've gone into all this is to show how everything all the demonic forces do, small or large, is for a grand scale purpose. And how, I believe, we truly can virtually connect each effort to either the antichrist's endeavors or the false prophet's because they together, in the end, usher in their father, Satan, as god.

So, where exactly does the spirit of python fit in to all of this? Especially since scriptural accounts only point to him being connected to the art of divination? How does this account for the other 'faces' of python?

The false prophet, as we discussed, through whatever means possible, ultimately lures mankind into corrupt spiritualism and false dependence on anything but the one true God. The false prophet's job is to replace the glorious Holy Spirit. The false prophet is on a mission to rid the face of the earth of true religion and squash everyone in his way. And because this is the totality of the false prophet's agenda, he is the overseer of every demonic prince and power who works against the lives of individual believers, who infiltrates the church to dismantle it - and the lives of the unsaved to corrupt them with false spirituality.

As far as the true church of God is concerned, he sends in spirits of Jezebel, spirits of witchcraft, etc., to crush us. And those captains of the guard (the "body" guards assigned to keep our "Body of believers" from growing in holy power) utilize the efforts of the thousands of spirits of idolatry, dissension, jealousy, insecurity, fear, self-pity, self-loathing, indifference, pride, bitterness, unforgiveness, addiction, sickness and disease, gossip, self-righteousness, poverty, hopelessness, impatience, intellectualism, religiosity, selfishness, etc. These all work on individuals separately to ensure that unity never transpires and then ultimately, strangulate the leaders and other strong presences of God in entire bodies - where they can get away with it.

Ultimately, both the individuals and the Body as a whole end up being suffocated, limp, and rendered breathless. They are divided and destroyed or in the least, powerless for Christ and just go through the motions. They don't grow or mature in truth and wholeness and especially, unity. They aren't winning souls and being used to change lives. Their voice is silenced to whatever degree. And so on and so forth.

This is what the python does to its prey. It renders its victim powerless and lifeless in every way. This is why I deduce that the spirit of python is one and the same as the false prophet; is the very embodiment or namesake that the false prophet took on all these millennia ago. He may accomplish this via false utterance or spirits of poverty or division or even Jezebel. Regardless, the end result is the victim is slowly constricted and rendered lifeless the way the natural python does to its victims.

If we observe children at play, we see (generally speaking) a little girl holding and nurturing her baby doll and a little boy tossing a ball or instinctively rolling his matchbox car across the floor. By nature, they are playfully imitating or "practicing" natural, God instilled behaviors. Men, being masculine, typically aspire sports, rough housing, or cars, while women typically aspire nurturing and other feminine behaviors. But the thing is, these behaviors are instinctive strictly because they are the way the Creator designed us. Likewise, interest in the supernatural realm is birthed out of God's design. Otherwise, we wouldn't desire to know our God and His wonders! However, it was the devil that took God's design and perverted it by instituting divination whereby mankind could rely on false gods in place of the real one. Worshiping God and getting your answers from the Holy One is God's design while having séances and reading tarot cards is Satan's design.

The point? Anything that is instituted by the devil is something he reigns over! So, even if we casually practice divination, or if a decision we make is fueled by fear rather than our confidence in God, for example, we are giving charge over to evil. And where he is in charge, the participants are subject. This is what we do not grasp. This is what we do not appreciate! Everything that goes on in this world is either of holy inspiration or of evil inspiration. We have got to stop thinking we are not exalting the devil or worshiping him just because we aren't Satan worshipers or witches! We lift him up every time we agree with his ideals and step on God's! We are so blind to how much honor we grant the evil kingdom. We must finally comprehend that when we participate in anything the dark kingdom institutes, including things like worrying or needing to get our own way, for example, we are willfully obeying his statutes, we are magnifying him, and we are subjecting ourselves to his authority. Because he is legally authorized to rule over everyone that agrees with him! And everything from blatant divination to unwittingly feeling sorry for ourselves is dark kingdom territory simply because the Almighty God NEVER set into motion the idea that anyone should be these ways.

Additionally, the empire, Operation Python, was necessitated out of idolatry to help Satan take over the world as god so the empire's strategy always revolves around bringing people into agreement with spiritual falsities and loving something, anything, more than Jesus. Satan's minions are out to create as many legal bridges into our lives by bringing us into agreement with his policies any which way they can. They must do this so that they can guide us in his evil direction down a destructive, defeated, powerless path. This is the counterfeit of how the HOLY SPIRIT guides us in His Holy ways down the path of righteousness, into victory and power! All we have to do is agree with and partake of whatever muck the false prophet offers. All these devil workers have to do is provoke us, tempt us, deceive us, WHATEVER IT TAKES to get us to abide by dark kingdom policies which always contradict God. They know that once they get our submission to their false ideals, they have a bridge into our lives and can dominate us. They can keep us from going higher in God and becoming all that we are called to. I don't care what it is. If we agree with anything that is instituted by the devil, or if we love anything more than God, we are idolatrous and abiding in the dark kingdom. This goes for the born again believer as well as the unsaved!

Let me reiterate that even if we give our hearts and lives to Jesus, if we exult anything over Jesus, it's that thing that really is our god! Seriously. We might think we've placed Jesus on the throne of our hearts but until we lay down everything that we love more than Him, Jesus is simply standing by... WAITING to take over as the Beautiful Lord He is... Waiting to bestow His all and all upon us.

And He will not force Himself on us. He might woo us, direct us to the truth, He may even whisper that He loves us into our ear. But He won't force us to put Him first. He is NOT like the devil who pushes and deceives his way into people's lives.

We truly cannot rely on or love anything more than the one TRUE God or we are in idolatry. And the false prophet is the author of false worship or reliance upon empty, worldly things or people! Whether you create an image, name it, set it on your shelf and pray to it for answers or you idolize something else and choose it to be your source of happiness in this life, you are exulting the false prophet because these are his rules. Please understand... if a person idolizes a relationship, a hobby, or material wealth, for example, and it's their source of satisfaction and hope above God, where so long as they have it they are happy, then it is a counterfeit, evil source because the institution of this false reliance came straight from the pits of hell. Since the materialism is not a true source of happiness, it's a lie. It's a false ideal, a false reality... Hence, a false god. And false gods are dominated by darkness. Demons possess and monopolize everything that is contrary to truth; everything false. False things are not of the natural earth kingdom or God's supernatural Kingdom. False things are strictly instituted by the kingdom of darkness. Therefore, the entities of that kingdom embody the falsities and use them as they please to accomplish their goals.

What is important to realize is that just because the false prophet clearly established his presence in the earth through The Oracle of Delphi called 'Python', we do not have to be seeking answers from homemade statues or a psychic to be loosing that same spirit of python in our lives. If we worship anything other than Jesus Christ, if ANYTHING is more to us than our Lord, is our source, our hope… we are doing the same thing as those who put their hope in the statues or psychic. And the false prophet, then, whether we like it or not, is our god.

My concluding but sobering thought concerning this is that because the false prophet established his vast platform and presence in our natural world via idolatry many millennia ago, this still surely must be his singular most effective strategy to maintaining power over those of us who have given ourselves to Christ. We must, therefore, do away with our idols and be like Paul. The Apostle was not overcome by even the sneakiest spirit of python because he was so one with our Lord and Savior, Jesus Christ - not idols. The false prophet could not break ground in Paul's life because his heart was consumed with truth and righteousness. There was no room in his heart for anything false because his heart was resolved for God. And just as the false prophet was powerless against Paul, he is powerless against anyone whose heart has a one track mind for Christ!

Things To Consider

If you were the false prophet with the astronomical mission to remove God's church and replace it with falisites, how would you go after and stifle "you"? What tactics would work to shut you down? ~If you can figure this out, I assure you, so has the false prophet. Now it's time to relinquish his access to these avenues.

Chapter Review Checkpoints

1. The woman in Acts 16 who practices soothsaying and was announcing that Paul and Silas were servants of the most High God is said to have been possessed by a spirit of python. If we were to speculate why any evil spirit would harass Paul and Silas at all, a most accurate conclusion would be

    A. so that they could get some evil kicks

    B. so that they could make their job difficult

    C. so that they could destroy Paul's ministry and shut it down

    D. so that they could tempt Paul to sin

2. Who was the actual source and identity behind the spirit of python's power back at the Oracle of Delphi?

3. If the false prophet was the true identity working through his namesake, python, who, then, was the entity working in Acts 16?

---

4. If the false prophet is the counterfeit holy spirit, despite taking on the namesake, Python, he is a very prominent and powerful entity whose sole mission is to dismantle the true church and promote false faith.
T or F

5. The Apostle Paul was a serious threat to the dark kingdom. The false prophet, therefore, attempted to connect himself to Paul via the soothsayer in hopes of eventually shutting Paul's ministry down. But, Paul saw right through the damsel and stopped the enemy in his tracks instead. He was not overcome by this sneaky plot because

    A. he was so one with our Lord and Savior, Jesus Christ.

    B. his heart was consumed with truth and righteousness.

    C. his heart was resolved for God

    D. all of the above

6 . The false prophet is powerless against a believer in Christ who

A. loves God with all their heart

B. serves God by volunteering

C. is born again

D. read the entire Bible a few times

7. When somebody loves God with their whole heart, they are resolved for God, they know Him and God's Spirit reigns in them. So, while they may still not be perfect and might falter, they are so close to God that the Lord will reveal what the devil is up to much like how Paul discerned that the spirit operating in the woman was evil.

T or F

ANSWER KEY - CHAPTER VI
1-C, 2-The False Prophet, 3-The False Prophet, 4-T, 5-D, 6-A, 7-

Chapter Seven
Dancing With The Devil

I want to share about the revelation the Lord gave to me in 1989 and 1990. Mind you, I hadn't heard of the spirit of python at that time nor did I have any understanding of the kingdom of darkness. Heck, I didn't know much at all about the kingdom of God! But, I had recently given my life to the Lord and God began dealing with me in a mighty way. I will share what happened but, again, understand that I had only partial revelation of what transpired through the years until this past decade when it all came together by the Holy Spirit.

Three months after meeting Jesus in 1988 I met another man and the short of it is he was unsaved. But I was still ignorant to God's ways. I did not know that God teaches us in His Word to not be unequally yoked. Regardless, the fact was even though I was newly saved which meant we were spiritually not equally yoked, my ways were very much still equally yoked with his at that time. This is important to understand. On one hand, even though I was a new creature in Christ, born into eternal life, I was still of the same programming and my old flesh had the upper hand because I wasn't grounded in a good church, didn't know anyone who knew God, and I never read the Bible. Therefore, my spirit was unequally yoked to the guy while my flesh was very matched with his. He was what I knew. His ways were what was familiar to me.

The spirit of python (which I was oblivious to at the time) saw that I had come to receive Christ as my Savior and, knowing better than me that I would want to serve

God in mighty, miraculous ways, the dark empire labeled me a dangerous convert. They knew that if I actually grabbed a hold of all the truth God offers that I would run with it and do great damage to the kingdom of darkness. Somehow, I believe the dark empire knew this even at my birth or prior to it because of how tormented I was inside as a child. At any rate, now that I was saved, the empire was put on red alert and they had to come after the seed of light that was now born into me. And they had to work diligently at keeping me from coming to really know this powerful God Who saved me so that I wouldn't become powerful in Him!

This was why the unsaved man came into my life. Yes, I believe it was arranged by the spirit of python to lure me down a wrong path. And it worked because I spent the next decade in and out of a dysfunctional relationship with him because of our different spiritual conditions. Unfortunately, my resolve was to make him like me instead of respecting that this was between him and God. Due to my dysfunction and severely tainted programming, I continued for years on the wrong path and experienced nothing but battles and heartache. Deep down we were each good people, but we were both unhealthy in our own ways and the python played on this and used us to keep each other on a path of demotion rather than promotion.

Despite the unhealthiness of the relationship that I recognized only months after meeting him, within a year I was pregnant so we decided to get a place together. I was so naïve as to what it meant to live my life for the Lord. I perceived that when I gave Jesus my life that I was going to Heaven and my job was to live to be a kind, good hearted person and that was pretty much all there was to it. I was unaware that I should put Him in charge of my life. How perfect that was for the empire. That was just how Python needed things to be and it was how he would aim to keep them! As far as going to church after I was born again and baptized, I went briefly but was scared off by messages that scolded us for wearing miniskirts and make-up. I believe that very well could have been the spirit of python at work within that church. He knew if he had the pastor preach like that on those things that I, being a newcomer and self-conscious without makeup, would not want to be a part of that church. And he was right. I already felt bad enough. Why go to church and be made to feel terrible for wanting to put make-up on? So, I stopped going and I, therefore, remained ignorant to the ways of God. Then I moved in with this man I was now pregnant out of wedlock ….and I began having strange dreams.

  The first one that I can recall, I was in a barn with three little children under my care. The doors were locked and I wandered around for quite a while trying to find a way out to no avail. Finally, the main door opened and I saw the devil enter the barn. I was not frightened. It was as though he was a familiar acquaintance. Immediately, I politely informed him, "You have to let us out of here." His reply? A calm but resounding, "No" and he turned and walked back out the door. I rushed to the door and it was locked again so I became furious and frantically began searching the barn for another way out. I was determined to find a way. He was not going to get away with this, I would surely find a way out! But nothing. I could not find a way.

  Soon after this dream I had another. The details escaped me. I cannot remember what went on. All I can recall is waking up distressed over losing again to the devil. I remember realizing this was the second time I had a dream about the devil having powerand control over me. And soon after that dream there was a third. In this one I entered the back door of somebody's home. There was a lady in the kitchen doing dishes in front of me. We chatted a moment but were interrupted as I noted there was noise coming from somewhere. It was music coming from the basement. I asked her what was going on and she said there was a party downstairs, to go ahead down if I wanted. But I said no because I truly didn't want to. Yet, I opened the basement door to peek with no intention of going down and as I'm standing there I see the devil at the foot of the stairs looking up at me. He said, "Come on down" and I said, "No thank you" and attempted to shut the door. Again, I was not frightened. He was familiar. At any rate, I couldn't shut the door and suddenly I saw him lift his arm and raise his hand towards me. Then suddenly the steps disappeared and I began floating down the darkened stairwell to him against my will. The next thing I knew I was dancing with the devil. I wasn't afraid. He wasn't torturing me or anything. He just simply had this invisible ability to keep me there. As I danced I thought, "Why am I dancing with the devil? I don't want to be dancing with the devil!!" But I could not leave. And I woke up.

Sometime very soon after having these dreams I began feeling convicted of living with my boyfriend out of wedlock. I didn't know the term 'convicted' until later but it was this conviction that led me to decide I needed to get out of that relationship since I couldn't marry him. So one month after the birth of my son (my second child) I left the unsaved man and decided I needed to find out more about the right ways of living. I took my two small children, got an apartment across town, and began to seek God and His ways. I found a church that didn't make me feel beat down because even though he taught the truth, the pastor was very loving about it. And I was allowed to wear make-up. Right soon after I began attending, the pastor was preaching about fornication. He taught that it was not God's way and that it wasn't good for us to do things contrary to the ways of the Lord. So, I came to understand why I was feeling it was wrong and realized God was personally stepping into my life to tell me to forsake this behavior. So, I repented and decided to no longer practice fornication. When I did, I felt something come alive in me!

It was good! And suddenly I wanted to know this God who had saved me. For the first time in my life I was compelled to find out more about the Jesus Who died for me. My curiosity had peaked. There was more to being saved than living a good-hearted life. God was more than an ancient character Who was far off in Heaven somewhere. God was personally with me, interested in me, and even 'talking' directly to me. For the first time in my life, I wanted to know this mighty Savior.

Immediately after I had this awakening in my soul to truth and rejected the wrong kingdom of darkness lifestyle, I had another dream about the devil. I cannot tell you what he was doing in this particular dream, how he was trying to control me, but I distinctly remember him being in my face overpowering me like the other dreams but I said to him, "No, you can't do that in the Name of Jesus" and instantly he SHRUNK to NOTHING right before my eyes! I sat straight up in bed and shouted, "I WON!"

That Sunday in church I told the pastor's wife (I wish I could remember her name) what had happened with all those dreams and now how I had won for the first time finally. I mean, indulge me for just a minute. You have to understand that all of my life I was the loser! If I ever did anything good, I was still the underdog. No matter what I did. Add to that the several dreams of direct defeat to the devil where I strived and fought to get out of his grip but to no avail. He always prevailed over me. But now…. He got in my face presuming his pre-existing power and BOOM, for the first time he is shrunk to absolutely nothing! Through the Name of Jesus (and because I wasn't in active submission to the devil) I was the victor! It was a most profound moment and I will never, ever forget it. So, in my enthusiasm I shared it with the pastor's wife and she said, "Paula, when you were living in sin, you WERE dancing with the devil. But when you turned away from that sin, the devil lost his power over you."

Whoa! That made sense! Suddenly I was on fire for God like never before. I knew there was a lot more to this Jesus than what meets the eye. So I began seeking Him and more of His ways. And the Holy Spirit opened my eyes. He spoke to the depths of my heart and further explained what the pastor's wife had said. He said that when we yield or say yes to sin, we are abiding in the kingdom of darkness (which is contrary to 'abiding' in God). This was when the Lord first revealed to me that there are two main governments far above any human governments and they were the kingdom of darkness and the Kingdom of God. And when you walk in agreement to any government by practicing its principles, by living a lifestyle consistent with that particular government's standards, it's like you are a citizen of that territory and it has authority over you. Even if you are just visiting. If you are an American citizen visiting England, while you are there, you are subject to England's authority by choosing to be there. If you violate English laws, the enforcement officers have the right to address you and you are obligated to submit. Just the same, fornication is a lifestyle promoted in Satan's government, in his kingdom. When you participate in Satan's kingdom, you place yourself in his jurisdiction.

The Lord cemented my understanding that I had been living in dark kingdom territory when I was willfully practicing fornication. And He said that even though I was redeemed that anytime I step into the dark kingdom by practicing ANY of the devil's ways, I put myself under his authority - whether I realize it or not. That's why I couldn't stop dancing with the devil even though I tried to! Apparently, during the barn dream, the barn I willfully chose to visit was Satan's territory. Only after I chose to be there of my own free will, Satan could lock me in if he wanted and I couldn't do a thing about it (outside of repent). He didn't drag me into the barn; I went there on my own. The same with the house I entered. Symbolically, the house represented Satan's territory because after willfully entering the premises, he had the ability to control me and make me go down to the basement to dance with him even though I didn't want to. The interesting thing is that in the final dream of the devil where I had won, I don't recall us being in a building. We were in open space because, thankfully, I was no longer in his territory. And when he tried to maintain his authority over me (because he will pretend he still has it even when he legally loses it) he was snuffed out at the name of Jesus!

Since I had rejected Satan's kingdom and stepped out of his jurisdiction, I wonder why he thought he could maintain his hold on me. Isn't it amazing that he's always hopeful of maintaining his power to the very end? The fact was, I had stepped out of his territory but he was still going to attempt to intimidate me and mess with my life until I showed him that I KNEW that Jesus, the ultimate authority, was the victor. And that was all it took. That's when he relented. All this to say it is paramount that we get out of the enemy's jurisdiction but it is equally paramount (only after we know we have stepped out of dark territory) to stand on the name of Jesus when the devil tries to stick around and play boss.

Let me add that it is not wise to attempt to use the name of Jesus, even if you are saved, if you are willfully hanging out in dark territory! Seriously! The devil will only laugh in your face. For real. I believe this is a serious mistake we believers make. We are told to take authority over demons because we received Jesus as Savior. Meanwhile we are the ones in their jurisdiction. And you simply cannot go on somebody else's property on their terms and tell them what to do. For example, it is illegal to use marijuana in the state of Pennsylvania even for medicinal purposes. The use of marijuana for medicinal purposes is legal, however, in the state of California. If you are a resident of California and use marijuana for medicinal purposes and take a trip to Pennsylvania and get caught 'taking your medicine', you are subject to Pennsylvania regulations and will be sanctioned accordingly. You cannot use the name of your state to claim exemption from PA law. Just the same, you cannot use the name of your Jesus when you are voluntarily participating in Satan's kingdom giving him authority.

But if you do find yourself on the 'wrong side of the law', all you have to do is genuinely get out of that dark territory by repenting and then the name which is above all names is legally applicable to protect you. Indeed, by our simply, but genuinely, repenting, renouncing, and rejecting whatever we are doing that is a part of Satan's government and stepping OUT of devil territory, we are stepping into the Kingdom of Might where, at the name of Jesus, every knee shall bow. And that's all it takes! It's that easy!

Or is it?

In a way, it truly is quite simple. Reject dark practices and instantly, you are "legally" out of dark government reign. Dark government enforcement officers (or spirits, rather) cannot *legally* arrest you (or torment you) if you are no longer in their territory any more than a Texas sheriff can arrest a criminal in Pittsburgh. So, in that sense, it's pretty simple. Unfortunately, it's not always easy to do.

When we have lived in a certain territory all or most of our lives, it's not easy to pack up and leave. Especially if we have generational ties to the place! Our roots run deep. We 'love' it there because it is what we are familiar and comfortable with. It is our way, it's all we ever knew. When this is the case, it's not easy to just leave what you know behind. It doesn't matter what the sin is. If it's a place you were born into, it really is a part of who you are.

This is what I spent the better part of the following two decades learning. Despite renouncing fornication, I fell back into it at different times. I was double-minded. For many a season I would be head strong for my Lord and His ways. Then suddenly I would be consumed with myself, my sorrows, my needs, my wants… my desires. And I would go after them first. Sadly, I occasionally found myself back in dark kingdom territory and suffering the consequences of it.

    I asked the Lord what I could have done differently; what I could have done to overcome the obsessive drive that occasionally possessed me and drove me into territories I knew better than entering. The biggest thing I heard the Lord telling me was I didn't just up and cross the boundaries of God's government into the devil's grounds all of a sudden. Rather, I had been inching towards the dark territory little by little and eventually, was too close to have any restraint left in me. God showed me that this happened because I would first fall away from feeding on His Word and focusing on Him, worshiping Him, and praying. After a while of starving myself of the light of God and His presence, His power was shoved to the side and the parts of me that were still programmed wrong began to take over again. The Lord pointed out that my lack of ongoing Holy scripture consumption was why I became weak to the leading of the evil one again. Because I didn't stay in the Word where I was being transformed and renewed, I fell away from the sanctification process and back into the sin process. By neglecting the life of the Word, I was vulnerable to the wiles of the enemy again and likely to regress back into old programming.

    Additionally, because negative thinking and low self-esteem (which were agreements to darkness that added to Python's hold on me) were still a part of my makeup at the time, the devil continually hindered my experience with other believers and I'd shrink away believing I was alone in this world. Had I instead reached out past the hurts to a genuine believer and sought prayer, their prayers may have helped me to rise back up and not fall far enough away where the devil had the ability to lure me back into my old bad habits or 'lifestyles'.

As you can see, there are several variables behind why a righteous man falls. For those of us who love God, it's not easy for the devil to lure us into wrong kingdom practices if we are saturated in the presence of God and His Word. So where the devil starts is by keeping us out of the Word of God because the Word truly is power. It is a life force with endless supply. It is literally transforming. If only I would have devoured the Word… Oh, how my life would have been so different.

Please… No matter where you are in your walk, no matter how long you have been walking with the Lord, if you are not devouring the Word and passionately seeking His Kingdom first, if He is not your primary focus and there is something else possessing you above God, please reach out to a mighty servant of Christ you can trust and ask for prayer and ongoing accountability. Then repent and cry out to Jesus to bring you to a right place in Him where you are delivered from your love of anything but Him. Travail and plead for the blood of Jesus to drive you to incessant hunger for Him and His Word above ALL THINGS. Plead for this with all you have in you so that you will not have to spend YEARS suffering at the hand of Python like I did. Even if dark clouds do not follow hard after you and the devil isn't taking advantage of your playing around in his territory and isn't shutting you down, you still will not be able to walk in the all and all of Christ! I cannot stress it enough. We must take a good hard look at our lives and if we see that it's our tendency to end up dancing with the devil when we don't wittingly choose to, then we need to renounce some things and pursue our God with vigilance. And we need renewed by the Word of God!

The devil is working relentlessly to keep us as far from all truth as possible. And regardless of our backgrounds, he's responsible for promoting all of our faulty programming, all of our emotional weaknesses, and all of our bad habits. And he knows exactly how to work us to keep us locked in them. But when we gave our lives to Christ, a power was born in us from on High that is able to help us overcome ALL of it! The only thing is we have to come into alignment with the power by seeking God, His ways, and His heart. And the only way to do that is by fervently praying, reading the Bible, and meditating on its precepts. Then, the Holy Spirit works with us to bring us to victory.

But we won't get there if we don't pray diligently and dig deep into the powerful Word of God.

If you are like me and lost a lot of years to defeat, don't fret. The good news is God is avidly working on our behalf to bring us the truth. You know, the Holy Spirit has literally been fighting for me, IN me, all these years to bring me out from under the python's rule! He has never given up on me and He never will. He loves me and is faithful to finish what He started in me! And the same goes for you!

But, the ball is still in our court. It truly is up to us to respond to the Lord's leading and take the steps towards a deeper relationship with our God and coming into a solid knowing of what His Kingdom entails so that we are reprogrammed and step completely out of dark kingdom territory. Please... Do not proceed any further in this book or anything else until you whole heartedly embrace that the measure the devil gets away with in our lives even after we receive Jesus as our Savior is ... UP TO US.

Things To Consider

Are you consistently focused on Your Lord, or is there a lot of wavering?

YES or NO

If you are struggling to focus on the Lord consistently, please confide this in a strong Christian friend who can pray for you and support you in this area. This is an imperative first step. And then cry out to the Lord. Confess the truth of your heart and ask Him to give you immense hunger for Him and His Word so that you will then be transformed!

Chapter Review Checkpoints

1. When we come to know the Lord, we are new creatures in Christ which means we have the Spirit of God born into us and a power from on High is then able to change us from the inside out. Does this transformation transpire instantaneously?

    A. Yes. The power of God in us causes us to never be tempted to sin again

    B. Yes. Once we repent and receive Jesus, all of our old ways and bad habits cease to exist.

    C. No. All of our programming is still the same

which is why we must read the Word of God and be transformed by the renewing of our minds.

D. No. But if we pray hard enough, God will change us.

2. When people are born again, the devil targets them if they are a potential threat to his dark kingdom. The devil will, therefore,

A. try to isolate the believer or lure them into idolatry

B. try to keep the believer in old, familiar territory where they will be likely to continue in their old ways.

C. try to keep the believer from focusing on God and reading the Bible as much as possible.

D. all of the above.

3. When we renounce the kingdom of darkness and step out of the devil's jurisdiction, he instantly loses legal authority over us but will still act as though he has it if we don't take authority over him through the name of Christ.
T or F

4. If we are saved by the Blood of the Lamb and we want to venture out a little into dark kingdom territory, we will be safe as long as we use the name of Jesus while visiting.
T or F

5. It is not always easy to step out of dark kingdom ways when we have practiced them our entire lives. Therefore, we must connect ourselves to strong believers who will pray for us and we must also cry out to the Lord to give us a hunger for Him that far surpasses any hunger we've had for anything else in our lives.

T or F

6. If you find yourself on the 'wrong side of the law' and suffering at the hand of Python, you can easily come out of his jurisdiction by

      A. genuinely repenting and renouncing what you've done

      B. continuing as you were but declaring to the false prophet that you are God's property

      C. rebuking Python in the name of Jesus

      D. all of the above.

7. You can get away with violating God's ways and practicing Satan's so long as you are saved and read your Bible every day.

T or F

8. Old programming plays a huge role in why we continue in sin after we are born again. But the way we undo the old programming is by being transformed by the renewing of our minds. We do this by devouring the _____ of God.

9. If we do not consistently feed on the Word and seek God with all of our hearts, we will prolong the sanctification process and will routinely fall into the same cycles of sin.

T or F

10. When we saturate ourselves with God's Word, we are empowered to walk in righteousness. If we miss reading the Word for a day, we don't instantly regress back to our old ways. But if we get away from reading the Word and focusing on God with our whole heart for any length of time, we are inching our way towards falling back into

A. old programming

B. dark kingdom territory

C. dark kingdom authority

D. all of the above

ANSWER KEY - CHAPTER VII
1-C, 2-D, 3-T, 4-F, 5-T, 6-A, 7-F, 8-Word, 9-T, 10-D

Chapter Eight
When You Seek Me With All Your Heart

Do we realize that if we are not seeking God with our whole hearts, when we are lukewarm or casual in making Him Lord of our lives, we are in the danger zone? Many of us accept Christ as our Savior but fail to build a close, solid relationship with Him. So, then, even after we think we've committed in our hearts to live for God, we're not really hiding under the shadow of the Almighty and the devil remains in authority. This (again) is why devouring the Word of God and praying without ceasing is imperative. It's the only way to come out of our old ways - and Python's grip.

I'm not going to apologize for this book not being about casting out demons but rather is primarily about our relationship with Christ. If you've picked up on that thus far, you are exactly right. My walk with the Lord was powerless and I was subject to dark forces because I was unwittingly idolatrous and I did not saturate myself in God's Word and presence. I'd go to church, serve in many ways, I was good hearted and didn't practice obvious sin most of the time. But I didn't know and understand God's precepts concerning many things. I didn't realize I had idols. And I certainly didn't know who I was in Him. Why? Because I wasn't in His Word which would have led me into these truths. Things would go wrong in my life and I would wonder why God's Word wasn't true. The fact was, His Word WAS true. I was the one who was not in alignment with what it said! I learned about casting out demons and breaking generational curses when I was a babe in Christ! But this did me little good because I didn't realize that God really wasn't first in my heart. Not only that, what good is breaking a generational curse that you are still operating in and unwittingly in agreement with? It's not really broken off if you still practice it! So, please embrace that what I am saying is the absolute truth. It's why many of us are yanked around by evil and powerless for God.

Like I said, the fact is after we give our lives to Jesus it is still likely that we will function according to our old nature and life-long programming. But all we have to do is daily take steps towards loving God first and with all of our hearts. If our heart acknowledges that it is corrupt except that God helps us to live right, and we desire to do right, God's grace abounds! Psalm 91 doesn't tell us that if we behave perfectly He will protect us. It says that if we dwell or abide in Him that He will protect us. Well, what does it mean to dwell or abide in Him? My understanding is that these terms reflect being in a fixed state of being. So I would deduce that abiding in God is being fixed on, or focused on, GOD. That's what it means to make Him our first love. If we think about it, whenever we love anything we are in fact fixed on it. It has our focus. So, Psalm 91 is saying that when we are fixed on God, when He is our focus, then many benefits, such as divine protection, will be ours! It's in this abode only where divine protection lies! So the bottom line is the spirit of python cannot harm us when God is our number one!

This is no grand revelation but loving God first isn't automatic. Through two plus decades of Christianity, I loved God but I loved other things as well if not more. I just couldn't see it because they were natural, good desires. In 1991 I had found a fantastic church and suddenly my life was all about getting to know my Jesus! And I was! Everything revolved around the Lord; my activities, my service, etc. But, a couple years into this, I experienced the Holy Spirit continuously speaking to me for a year and a half that if I'd seek Him I would find Him if I'd seek Him with all my heart. What?

I was confused because I was very involved and active in my church, serving and deliberately choosing God's ways. My life was completely different and I was on the right track for the first time ever. But I grew frustrated because He kept reiterating this to me for a year without explanation, "Paula... If you seek Me, you will find Me when you seek Me with all your heart..." until one day in 1994 I was face to face with my rebellion.

Let me tell you what happened...

After two and a half years of proactively getting to know and serving the Lord with all I was, I had a vision. I was lying down to go to sleep when suddenly I saw this torso, like a statue of a bust from the neck to the belly. The bust had a zipper about eight inches long on it and this hand had the zipper opened to about the ¾ mark. Next, I saw the zipper was fully opened and the hand reached in and took out this black, ugly heart. Then the same hand put a brand new, beautiful heart in its place. I said, "What is going on?" because I didn't realize I was having a vision right away. Suddenly, I heard, "I am about to remove something ugly from this person and replace it with something new and beautiful." In my brilliance, I declared, "Of course, that's what You do with everyone who is born again. You give them a new heart." And the Lord said, "Look at the first picture" (how elementary) and suddenly I saw where the zipper was opened ¾ of the way. The Lord said, "I have been opening this person for three years and when they are fully open, I will remove something ugly from their heart. But then I will replace it with something beautiful."

That was all He said. I wasn't sure what it meant. I drew some conclusions, of course, but the understanding wasn't given for nearly a year.

The truth is I had begun seeking the Lord the best I knew how starting in March of 1991. I had this vision in the fall of 1993. Come March 1994, something came over me at precisely the three year mark. I had had enough. I had been waiting for God to send me a Christian husband and father for my two children for three years. But nothing. Not even so much as a date! Every year that passed was another year my children had grown without the influence of a Godly father. I knew what it was like to grow up without a good male role model so I was desperate for my children to have one. As far as I was concerned, every day that went by without their having this Christian man in their lives was a day lost and I dreaded every single one of them. I had desired this Christian man so deeply for so long that not getting him was finally getting the best of me. I was suddenly so discontent with my life at my church because, unlike 98% of the rest of the congregation, I was single and had children with no father. I hated this so badly. I still remember the pain of it to this day. So, what I ended up doing was leaving my apartment and life and church behind and went back to my ex-boyfriend (my son's father). I decided (and even had the audacity) to inform my pastor that I would be a good Christian influence on my ex and we would get married right away so that I wouldn't live in sin. Boy, was I delusional!

And that's what I did. Of course, I moved back to his area in - you guessed it - his house! PRIOR to getting married, too! Oh, I scurried to try to put a wedding together to make things 'legal' but the wedding was not happening fast enough. In fact, we began having problems before I even had the chance to pull it off. And you are guessing right if you're assuming I fell back into sexual sin.

Within five months I was pregnant… again.

The troubles increased by the month between us and things really started to go bad. My car suddenly broke down and I had no money to fix it. I had lost my job because of the dysfunction of our relationship. I was hedged in and had no way out. I reached out to welfare to try to get out of there and back on my feet but they denied me because I was still with him. I wouldn't lie, like I've seen so many do, and say that I wasn't living with him so that I would qualify for assistance. So, I was broke and destitute. I couldn't even go to the doctor concerning the pregnancy because I had no medical coverage.

We began fighting so relentlessly because I wanted to leave him but had no way to do so and he wouldn't help me. I was literally trapped there. And I would not pray about it for a couple of reasons. One, I knew I was in a bad way but two, I blamed God. I felt it was His fault that I was in the situation because He hadn't given me a Christian husband. So, I was angry with Him - even to the point of cussing at Him!

At any rate, I wouldn't pray, I refused to read my Bible, and I certainly bypassed all Christian television shows if I came across them. I was too angry. But, my Dear, precious Lord Who loves me so amazingly, tricked me into watching a particular program on Christian television. I stumbled on this show where this couple was talking about their infertility. It grabbed my attention because I was pregnant. Suddenly, the couple began sharing how they experienced a miracle from God and ended up getting pregnant. That's when I realized what God had done but by now, I was interested and kept on listening. It was a touching program but the pivotal moment happened at the end when the host said, "It doesn't matter WHAT you've gotten yourself into, God can get you out of ANYTHING! Just repent and surrender and He will help you."

At that, my heart broke and I began bawling my eyes out. I felt that even after all of my wretched ugliness, my God still loved me! He hadn't tricked me into watching the show so that He could beat me over the head with a Bible and scold me with scriptural truths like I had thought. Rather, He tricked me so that He could reach His hand out to me, way down to the bottom of the pit I was in. He wasn't scolding me. He was rescuing me from the mess I had gotten myself into.

My response? I said, "There's that scripture!" and that was it. I thought it was peculiar but I did nothing about it. In fact, I chose to not watch the rest of the program on television and I went to lie back down for a while. I decided I would get some more rest and then seek God when I woke up. And that's what I did. I woke up around 10:30 and after going to the bathroom and such, I went back to the couch, picked up my Bible, turned on the television and opened my Bible and low and behold, the EXACT same thing happened. Here, the Christian station was re-airing the same show from only three hours earlier and I happened to turn it on in the exact moment they put that verse up on the screen. And sure enough, my Bible was opened to the exact same page!!! I am not kidding! It freaked me out! So I said, "What, Lord? What is it about this scripture??? You hounded me about this for over a year and now here it is! What are you trying to tell me?"

The next day was very interesting. I mean, the fact was I was still stuck there in that bad situation. So, after I got my daughter off to first grade and my son off to Headstart, it was about 7:40 am. and I sat down on the couch, picked up my Bible off the coffee table and the remote control to the television, and as I flipped open my Bible I, at the same time, turned on the television and low and behold, I see covering the television screen, Jeremiah 29:13.... "If you seek Me, you will find Me when You seek Me with all your heart". And honest to goodness, I looked down at my Bible and there it was, also! And not because the page was bookmarked or opened to it a lot! I only looked at that verse in my Bible a few times during that year. The Lord had been speaking it to me through other resources.

Instantly, the vision of the torso popped into my mind and the Lord said, "Remember how I told you I was going to remove something ugly from this heart?" and I said, "Yes, I do" and right away I had understanding. It was an idol. It was "my" idol. It was my idolatry!

The Lord showed me that for three years I had been seeking Him but my heart was divided. He said that it is okay to have the desire for a husband because that is His desire for me, too. But He said He had to show me that it meant more to me than He did. So much so that I was willing to leave the wonderful church and church family He had blessed me with. I was willing to step out of His ways in order to acquire what I wanted, that I would take things into my own hands despite Him. The Lord showed me that if, in place of the torso vision, He'd have told me that my desire for a husband was an idol that I wouldn't have believed it. He had to allow me to come to my end. So, from March of 1991 when I began to get to know the Lord, God deliberately didn't allow me to even date by keeping men from approaching me so that He could expose what was hidden in the depths of my heart. And it took EXACTLY three years - just as He said.

The truth of it in a nutshell was that my desire for a Christian mate was idolatrous because it meant more to me than God. This is the type of thing that is very difficult to recognize in ourselves at times. And it's a powerful tool the false prophet gladly uses.

The problem was that since the preoccupation of my heart was a good and natural thing, especially concerning my babies, I had no reason to suspect it was bad and is why God had to let me come to my end and expose it in order for me to believe the truth. I couldn't understand why He kept telling me over and over that if I'd seek Him I would find Him if I'd seek Him with all my heart until my actions proved what was at my core! Because over the course of the three years, my frustration and longing grew hotter and hotter until the day came I left my church and church family to go after this false god on my own terms.

The bottom line to disconnecting from the kingdom of darkness is loving God first and with all our hearts. But we can't assume giving our lives to Christ means we'll instantly love Him perfectly. Or that we'll no longer love other things more. I believe the beginning to truly falling in love with God is being able to confess the raw truth of our hearts - that we don't necessarily love him first. It's not like He doesn't already know, after all. But it takes OUR knowing and confessing to get anywhere. My not realizing that God wasn't really my top priority proved to be very dangerous for me (and my children, too!) despite living those three years revolving around the church in sincere servitude. But knowing is freedom. Please recognize and be willing to admit to yourself and God if and how much you love something more than God. Face it and simply surrender it. Don't feel guilty. Just confess it and move on. If you aren't sure if there's something above Him, just ask. And then determine to pursue Him even while your flesh is demanding its own way. Sooner or later, you'll truly love Him with your whole heart!

More so, please realize the quality of our relationship with God matters. Just as it would with any close friend, it takes effort to build a trusting, love relationship with the Lord. You have to spend time with Him. You have to get to know what matters to Him and honor it in order to demonstrate that you love Him. You also have to show affirmation and gratitude in order to establish that you value Him.

If you've built a love relationship with your spouse but suddenly you ignore them more and more, no longer noticing what makes them special or acknowledging the wonderful things they do... If you continually doubt them and reject their input on matters, or could care less about what is important to them, just how close will you remain? It's the same with God. If we treat Him these ways, just how intimate really are we with Him?

If this is an eye-opener for you and you're recognizing your negligence, don't lose heart! As I said, all it takes is the desire to build that relationship and all of a sudden, because you are focused and yielding, the Lord will become your number one. No need to stress thinking the proof of your abiding is in your victory over sin or how well you can quote scripture. The proof is when we are truly desiring God first. Just start each day proclaiming that God is first and seek Him and His righteousness and you are thereby nurturing your relationship with God.

But also understand that it's a daily decision because the devil has been strategically working in each of our lives since our youth to pollute us. He's put false ideas into our belief system, tainted our thought and reasoning processes with wrong programming, and ensnared us into sin and wrong physical, emotional, and mental habits. So we will likely start out in our relationship with Jesus torn between Him and our previous loves. And let's face it - we've loved our previous loves for a very long time. We all know that breaking up is hard to do. And Jesus knows this which is why He patiently deals with us despite His jealousy.

Not to mention, the Bible does say that our spirit and flesh are at war. Since birth, our flesh has had a one track mind concerning gratification. All our flesh knows is its interest in feeling good. It wasn't born into this world chasing down opportunities to be strained or denied, exerted and in the very least, humbled. Mix that with the fact there is an evil empire in our midst that uses our flesh to bring us into covenant with him and we can soberly say that we are, indeed, at war.

So since Satan's goal is to become god of all the earth in very literal terms, he takes advantage of this warring going on in us and faithfully plays his part in keeping us locked in our flesh so that our spirits cannot soar. He begins to download our flesh with wrong things in our youth. And then he will do as much damage to us as possible very early on - as much as he has legal ability to. The false prophet empire will cause discouragements and where he can get away with it, he'll see to it we are mistreated, rejected, or hurt somehow through abuse (verbal, emotional, physical, sexual), bullying, abandonment, neglect, etc. The more the wrong ideals or garbage the enemy downloads into a child and the deeper the wrong programming goes, the greater foothold he acquires, and the greater the wedge he hopes to place between the child and the one true God. Remember, he is all about being god himself which means his entire mission is to dethrone the real God from our lives. So, the false prophet assigns a specific set of demons to a child's life to pollute him as much as possible before the child even has the chance to seek the truth. And unfortunately, the demons get away with a great deal because the parents and their forefathers were not grounded in truth themselves and are, often times, the ones who opened the doors and gave rights to the dark kingdom.

  Then Satan counts on the fact that, should the day come that a person discovers Jesus, they'll have too many barriers and chains to press into Christ with all their mind, soul, and strength. Finding and submitting to Jesus doesn't mean all the false ideals, habits, wrong thinking and such will magically disappear. What has changed is now we have the Glory in us to be transformed by the renewing of our minds. We are no longer bound to the old programming, habits and sin because of the power that was born into us. We are free to put on the mind of Christ now. Unfortunately, we don't always realize this and either we are lax in pursuing a close relationship with God and releasing the power of God from within us or we're too distracted to realize He really isn't number one. Especially when we are passionate about our own agenda and are boggled down with idols, soul wounds, and false ideals. When we become born again, Satan suddenly has to compete to maintain or regain our submission to him and all the wrong ideals he placed in us over the years. If he doesn't get away with stealing the Word from us or choke it out of us with the weeds of life, he'll use the grounds he already set up in our lives since childhood. And he'll work tirelessly to do this! This was why, soon after I was born again, I met an unsaved man who was exactly what I knew in my past. Satan had to lure me back into familiar territory and keep me operating according to his wrong kingdom ways. This was how he would maintain his authority over me and keep me powerless.

At that time in my life, there were so many aspects of me that were not in line with truth. First, I was raised that premarital sex was normal. It's what people did. Next, I had been sexually molested so I became completely dysfunctional in my sexuality. I also had deep seeded shame, low self-worth, and felt like ruined goods. I unwittingly grew up seeing myself as inferior. Perceiving myself these ways was contrary to scripture which says I was fearfully and wonderfully made! That was the devil's plan because it caused me to see myself as less throughout my youth and much of my adult, "born again" life - which was contrary to the truth! The lie Satan instilled in me was so deeply rooted and real to me that I was unable to see and believe God's view which was the correct one - despite knowing He saved me from sin and death. I never even considered that there was another way of viewing myself. God had to drill this into me! The reflection I saw in the mirror was always ugly even if I fixed it up as nicely as I possibly could. I hated myself. And this is not of God's Kingdom! Hating yourself is instituted by evil. So, even up until a couple years ago, I was walking in the wrong kingdom and ruled by Python because deep down I despised myself! I just didn't realize it. Nor did I realize it was a dark kingdom policy that subjected me to dark kingdom jurisdiction! To this day I STILL hear the spirit of python's suggestion that nobody 'really' loves me; that I'm ugly and no good or not good enough. But because I'm being transformed by the Word like never before, I'm on to the enemy and I'm doing better about bringing every bad thought into the obedience of Christ. My strategy is the moment I feel a bad feeling in the flesh no matter what type or what it is related to, a red flag goes up that the devil has a minion trying to bring me into a bad place so that he can access my life. Bad feelings do not exist in the Kingdom of God because there is nothing bad there. And if I am now a citizen of a Kingdom where there is nothing bad at all, I no longer have to embrace or possess bad things! I am free from all of them. Bad things are not an ingredient to Holy Kingdom living! So, I therefore do not have to receive the bad feeling or thought, much less hold on to it and let it take up residency! The result is I am no longer in mental covenant with the wrong kingdom! And Python no longer has a legal right over me in this area.

But back to topic, the spirits in my childhood caused me to feel small and inadequate. The devil knows a child needs affirmation and to be believed in, for just a couple examples, so if he can steal these from a child he will, because it literally secures him a throne in that child's heart. He knows if a child is emotionally neglected and not valued that he'll have a huge doorway into that child's core through which to rule him/her even if that child grows up and one day says yes to Jesus. He knows it will hinder that child's ability to perceive God's love.

So do you see better now why the enemy has to hurt, twist and pollute us as many ways as he can as early on as possible? So that he has as many footholds as possible throughout our adult lives! And if the devil cannot get to a child through abuse or rejection because the parents are too loving and such, he'll look for other ways. Perhaps he'll cause the parents to get wrapped up in other wrong practices such as promoting self, materialism, or pleasure because if he's in with the parents, he's in with their children in like manner. If the spirit of python gets dad hooked on pornography, drugs, or alcoholism, the same spirit is allowed to begin to work on the children. If the spirit of python can get mom hooked on fortune telling, the feminine rights movement, or gossip, that same devil can work on the children. You get the idea.

And for those seemingly perfect households where church going has always been the family tradition and the devil can't get a hold on the parents as easily through obvious sin, no problem. He'll simply play on their pride or flesh and try to implement, for example, the spirit of control - better known as the spirit of witchcraft - whereby (if even subtly) manipulation, domination, and intimidation are what is practiced in the household. Or better yet, he'll attack their faith structure. The devil will speak lies that will keep them from coming into accurate understanding of scripture and the full truth of God. Or he'll promote a prideful, legalistic, religious or works related faith that completely defies the very gospel they supposedly follow.

Are you thinking I'm stretching it, here??? Think about it.... How many "Christians" don't believe the gifts of the Spirit are for today? How many still think they have to earn God's approval through works? How many sit in the pews week after week not really serving God and are spiritually dead and going nowhere? How many Christians claim to trust God but when you get down to it, are the ones completely steering the car themselves? How many different denominations are amongst us - along with the pride each one possesses which insists it is the right one! Need I go on? These are ALL lies instituted via Operation Python to keep the Church down and in disarray! The false prophet is behind everything false in the church! He employs whatever works in every believer's life to accomplish his agenda! Isn't it time we wake up?

Because man is fallen and sin is our nature, the devil works diligently beginning in our childhoods to set himself up in our hearts. Then, if we ever should respond to the call of Christ, he still has a chance at keeping us locked in to serving his government so that we will hopefully never seek God with our whole hearts.

<u>Things To Consider</u>

Have you recognized that you do love certain things in your life more than God? If yes, please quickly jot them down and then pray something like the following:

Gracious, Heavenly Father,

You do love me with an everlasting love, and I'm so very thankful for this. But Father, I realize… I do not love you with all of my heart. I realize, now, that I love ____ more than I should because I love it more than You! Father, this is not how I want to be. I confess it is idolatry and I repent! And I give this idol up to you. Father, I know I'm obsessed with or addicted to this. It has a hold on me. But, Father, You are with me and can help me overcome this and I know You will. Please lead me in Your Word so that I will find the right scriptural truths to cling to which will reprogram me and bring me into victory over it. Because this thing I love really isn't my all and all like

YOU are! Nothing compares to You! Just please help me to grasp this at the depths of my soul, Lord. Help me to tear down every wrong stronghold which sets itself between You and me. Give me incessant hunger for Your Word and deliver me from mental strongholds which are contrary to Your truth! You are the Way, You are the Truth, and You are the Life! I will come to You Father through Your Son Jesus And I will seek You, and I WILL find You! Because I WILL seek You with ALL of my heart! Amen.

Chapter Review Checkpoints

1. We are in a danger zone and vulnerable to the devil's tactics if we

    A. are lukewarm; neither hot or cold for God

    B. are casual about our pursuit of the things and ways of God

    C. are not seeking God with our 'whole' heart

    D. all of the above

2. We are called to have a relationship with God which entails

    A. repenting of our sins and receiving Jesus as Savior

    B. spending time talking and listening attentively to the Lord, admiring and affirming Him, showing appreciation and gratitude for all that He is to us

    C. seeking Him, finding out all we can about Him, knowing Him and what He is all about; knowing Him intimately

    D. all of the above

3. In order to have God's protection, we are to abide in God which means

    A. perfectly doing everything He says to a T

    B. being fixed on or focused on God and His Kingdom above all else

    C. going to church and telling everyone we are Christians

    D. rebuking the devil every time potential danger arises

4. If God is our focus because we love Him with our whole heart and we are, therefore, abiding in Him, then the spirit of python has no legal rights against us.
                                    T or F

5. We can be very busy doing Godly things and loving God genuinely yet still have a divided heart where a part of us loves something so much that it hinders our ability to focus on God; and may even compel us to walk away from God to attain it.

T or F

6. Satan inundates us in our youth with wrong thinking and abuse where he can get away with it so that we have deep wounds which make it difficult to believe the truth about ourselves. But if we find and truly submit to Jesus, all the false ideals, habits, wrong thinking will magically disappear.

T or F

7. God loves us and says we are fearfully and wonderfully made. Therefore, if we perceive ourselves in any negative fashion, we are in agreement with

    A. reality

    B. God

    C. the liar

    D. the entire world

8. Since we are citizens of the Kingdom of God where nothing bad exists, we no longer have to embrace or possess

A. offenses

B. rejection or abuse

C. negative ideas

D. all of the above

9. Satan uses these wounds to put a bigger wedge between us and God. Sometimes it's even difficult to comprehend God's love.
T or F

10. There is lifelong programming that needs transformed in us when we first come to Christ but it will happen if we pursue God with all we are and put Him first in our lives.
T or F

ANSWER KEY - CHAPTER VIII
1-D, 2-D, 3-B, 4-T, 5-T, 6-F, 7-C, 8-D, 9-T, 10-T

Chapter Nine
Confounded By Constriction

Just as it is that the physical python constricts and suffocates its prey to death, the spiritual python functions in much the same way. A spirit of python will coil around its victim causing them to lose their breath at first and eventually, paralyze them. Most often, the victim is unaware that they are being supernaturally constricted. They view their symptoms as natural occurrences, like feeling tired or apathetic. But there are rare occasions where people will literally feel the physical pressure wrapped around them restricting their breathing and rendering them immobile or experiencing suffocation. Whether the person physically recognizes the presence of the supernatural force which is constricting them or not, the end result is virtually the same.

Constriction is accomplished differently depending on the particular python spirit working. One spirit might paralyze its victim over a period of time, rendering them weak and foggy minded so that what they really feel and believe concerning truth is lost within themselves somewhere. Another spirit might come upon its victim out of nowhere and accuse them of being too inadequate for the task at hand, for example, and they'll stop dead in their tracks. They literally feel frozen or paralyzed in the moment. Meanwhile, a spirit of procrastination may come upon somebody as well, for example, suggesting to them that it's not time to speak up yet or that they should wait for a better time. Then of course, there is the spirit of laziness. It goes without saying that this spirit simply does whatever it takes to cause its victim to feel lazy and indifferent about following through with that which the Lord instructs them to do. Not to mention the spirits of fear or intimidation or witchcraft that might attempt to immobilize someone as well.

While these spirits of python are all different in their approach, we can see how they're all indicative of constriction. These various spirits know which works best on who they are assigned to so the symptoms of constriction will vary from person to person. Regardless of which, the end result if we are unaware of what is going on and not hiding under the shadow of the Almighty, is we'll end up lethargic, mute, powerless and often times, isolated.

Looking back over my youth, I can say I was very much a victim of constriction. My mind was extremely paralyzed, I couldn't think straight. I couldn't fathom the future. I could barely fathom the next day. As a student I got good grades but I was in a slight comatose state. I say slight because I was physically there, I participated, I excelled at times in certain things. But there was some sort of fog around my mind all the time. I felt separated from the other children and what I was doing, even from my own friends to a point. It was like I was only half there or on the outside looking in.

And then certain circumstances arose in my life in my teenage years that sent me into a more pronounced comatose state. A couple of times it was so deep that I couldn't even get out of bed. I'd sleep and sleep and sleep for weeks. Suddenly, even being a good student was lost to me because I couldn't get myself to school. I was severely depressed. I was numb. I was void of energy and life. I literally felt like I was a living 'dead' person. I'd spend any waking moments considering how I should take my life because not being able to move and live was humiliating. And the condition seemed unchanging even if it got a little better, I was still a very heavy ladened, hopeless person.

But while these intense seasons of despair which were full of drama seem they should claim great significance, I'd have to say that seeing how the same fog was on me even in my elementary years to the lesser degree is the more significant. I do not like remembering my childhood. While there certainly were moments of joyous experiences, my state of mind was always so far away because I was ladened with shame and self-hatred. I always had dreams that paralyzed me in the darkness of the night. The spirits which dominated me and my life were many and caused me to feel so small that I was only half alive.

The biggest way they worked directly against me was by setting up a throne in my mind; in my thinking. They taught me early on to feel sorry for myself when nobody affirmed how I felt or didn't believe in me. They taught me that this was because nobody ever really loves anyone in this world. Everyone is only out for themselves and is incapable of genuinely loving others. I was confused by this because on occasion I would witness other children seeming to be so precious to their parents. Their parents seemed to be on their side. They listened to them - or at least pretended to - and then they validated what their children said no matter how irrelevant or insignificant it was. I wondered what that must have felt like. I wondered if they even believed it was real or if they, too, understood that it couldn't possibly be because nobody is capable of really loving another.

So, the programming was solid and the enemy was diligent to start early on and to keep plugging away until it was so cemented that it was my response to everything. I am embarrassed to share this, but I recall a time when I was about eight or nine years old and something happened that I felt shunned again; not believed in or loved. I was so violently angry that I turned it inward and with tears of fury streaming down my face and pressing very hard, wrote on numerous slips of paper, "I am a pig!", "I hate myself!" and

"I am ugly!". Then I taped them all over my bedroom wall. I despised myself. I felt that if nobody else 'really' loved me that I shouldn't either. And I believed this with every fiber of my being. This was how much control the enemy already had over my mind, thinking, and emotions.

As I grew, so did the reasons to believe nobody really loved me because the enemy provided them faithfully. I have to confess it has only been within the last few years that the Lord revealed this part of the spirit of python's works in my life. I find it peculiar because this was the more profound grip he had on me. Not only had it been about programming my mind, but the devil had solidified the programming within my soul. Meaning, even when I began to be transformed by the renewing of my mind throughout my Christian walk and began comprehending that God really did love me, that He was for me, my soul wounds were so deep that my 'being' couldn't comprehend such information. Yes, my spirit chose to embrace the truth, but the truth quietly conflicted with what my soul knew and believed. And what my soul knew was that God had never intervened. He allowed every violation and injustice. When I was up against three attorneys in the judge's closed chambers at 16 years old, and I was interrogated for three hours concerning my allegations against those who sexually molested me, I was hung out to dry. I was, ironically, the one on trial! When both the physical abuse charges (which were backed by evidence via photos and a police report) and the sexual abuse charges were dropped for no good reason and there was no justice, where I was all alone in the ugly mess being called a liar... the Lord never showed Himself. To this day, the official end result of the matter was either I lied or invented it all in my insanity.

So, not seeing God ever once in that and the many other attacks brought against me, I realize that my soul had not believed that God really does care to help me, protect me, come to my aid. What I needed to do, then, was to tear down those strongholds and declare the truth to my soul, that God really IS for me, that He DOES care, and that He WILL avenge me. He will make all things right.

God showed me through a supernatural experience in 1992 that He really was for me, that He was angry at the enemies who were working against me. Unfortunately, while this did serve to send the message to my depths that God was for me, it didn't revolutionize my soul. It has taken all these years to identify that my soul wounds have always caused me to doubt this truth. I didn't even know what soul wounds were or that I should tear them down until a few years ago. But now that God has brought me to this level and I have been able to recognize that I had them, I have been able to tear them down and reject their validity. I have come to terms with the real truth that they were false, they were lies. Because I really am loved amazingly. And even though mankind fails each other by not loving perfectly, it doesn't mean I am less because of it. That I have no value. It doesn't mean I have to feel uttermost devastation and hopelessly alone in the world! It doesn't mean I should hate myself! It is so good to be FREE from such bondage!

But you see, while doing things according to kingdom of darkness governance puts us in dark kingdom jurisdiction in those moments, it's all the more challenging when dark kingdom territory actually sets up residency in OUR MINDS and SOULS. When the devil plants his throne in our thinking, this gives him a more personal and profound hold over us! So, even after I found Christ and learned of His love, that evil throne still dominated my mind and perspective and ruled over me.

If the devil can train our minds to go into specific, wrong thinking processes, he's in control. I wish it were possible to outline every single wrong thinking process the spirit of python would employ but I think we can sum it up simply. Since the Lord's Kingdom is good, is all loving, is hopeful, is light, is pure, then it is safe to say that any thinking pattern that is not in conjunction with these is from the devil's kingdom! So, what we need to do is continually be on the alert and pay attention to where our mind goes, what patterns it takes, how it reacts even in thoughts that we don't speak out loud necessarily. If we take a conscious look at our thinking and assess every single aspect of it, determining if it is of the Kingdom of Light or otherwise, then we would be able to begin recognizing the nature of the spirits that have set these strongholds up in our minds and souls. And then we can tear them down. We can take them captive and bring them into the obedience of Christ!

Philippians 4:8 (KJV) "Finally, brethren, whatsoever things are true, whatsoever things are honest, whatsoever things are just, whatsoever things are pure, whatsoever things are lovely, whatsoever things are of good report; if there be any virtue, and if there be any praise, think on these things."

That means DON'T think on ANYTHING contrary!!! Reject every bad thought! I would venture to say that even when people wrong us that we do not have to spend time meditating on it. If it hurts, deal with it accordingly and quickly, being careful to halt the festering of bitterness, jealously, animosity, all of it. If God tells us to take every thought captive and also tells us to think only on things that are lovely, then that includes thought flows that result from irritations, annoyances, offenses, or full blown violations!

We need to remember that we are of a royal priesthood. We are citizens of a mighty, HOLY Kingdom where there is no bad blood, no pain. We do not have to respond to the things or people in this world as though what they have to offer (good OR bad) is eternal. The way I am finally looking at things is that if something has no eternal value, then it essentially has zero value. So, why allow the idiosyncrasies of life to play significant roles??? The more we forbid empty and especially evil things from holding weight, the more the python has NOTHING to use to constrict us!!!

Prophet Kim Clement has spoken significantly about the spirit of python. This is where I learned the interesting notion that the spirit of python detects its prey much like the physical python does. Prophet Kim explained that the natural python doesn't see or hear very well and actually detects its prey with its tongue through its victim's movement and stirring of the dust. He said that it's the same spiritually. As humans, we come from dust and Prophet Kim teaches that when we are being noisy in our flesh (by being carnal, sinful, and operating out of flesh as opposed to spirit), that's when the spirit of python can detect us and move in. And while blatant sin stirs the dust up extremely well and makes us detectable, so do the little things such as self-pity, for example. Self-pity is one of the devil's policies, not God's. And many of us grow up trained to feel sorry for ourselves when something goes wrong and we are unaware that this is not of God's government, but Satan's. So, if this is a wrong program in somebody who is suddenly seeking Christ, all the devil has to do is create a scenario that will send the person into feeling sorry for himself and before you know it, the dust is all stirred up and the spirit which otherwise cannot see you can now sense right where you are and is (legally) able to move in to constrict. Perhaps through isolation or depression. It could be any number of things. But do you see the strategy here? First the devil has to tempt a person to stir up their dust which then gives him a door. The false prophet knows each person's weak spots and will always play on them. ~Our soul wounds are his treasure box!

Is it fair to say, for those of us who routinely feel sorry for ourselves, that we should just get over it already? I mean, we think we are feeling the way we do because we have to defend ourselves because we don't want to be treated unfairly or whatever. That it makes sense to acknowledge every single aspect of where others do us wrong because it is flat out uncalled for. But that is all baloney. Really. None of us deserve anything good. Everything we have and are is an unearned gift. What have we ever done to even merit the right to breathe? Who says life has to be "fair" when we never even earned the right to live at all? It's all poppycock. The only thing feeling sorry for ourselves serves is evil! We must face this and face it now!

As I said, because the devil had all kinds of authority over my household when I was a child, he was free to and did well to overload me with shame, hopelessness, and self-loathing. And I believe those states of my soul became connected to specific spirits of hopelessness and self-loathing that were attached to me at the hip which became like best friends and served to infiltrate my life circumstances and keep me defeated. The reason I refer to them as being like best friends is because a few years ago when the Lord exposed them, specifically the spirit of self-loathing, it's difficult to explain but it was such a familiar, comfortable part of me that I welled up with tears when choosing to renounce him from my life. You see, when that spirit influenced my circumstances via rejection or some violation which hurt, I'd regress deep into myself, into this dark safe place where nobody else could hurt me. Self-pity and self-preservation were my source, my strong tower, and it felt good to hide there. (Now I finally know to hide in God instead). I wouldn't want to be with anyone, talk with anyone, trust anyone, etc. This was my refuge. Even though this was where I thrived in self-hatred and loathing, it was the territory where I was in control (or so I thought). So, when I discovered what was going on and saw how this spirit was working and playing me with the things it routinely whispered into my ears, I chose to repent of my agreement with it and reject it out of my life. But in doing so, I was saying goodbye to a part of who I had been for 40 years! I felt like I was cutting a piece of my own heart out! And it wasn't easy. I had to look hard at the truth. I had to be resolved that I didn't want to behave like that anymore. That for as much as it 'felt good' to have that as my recourse that it was a destructive, lying part of who I had been. No matter how much (false) comfort it gave me. I had to be strong and follow through to where I really no longer permitted myself to go there. It was tough. In one minute I was cutting the spirit from my life, the next minute I was tempted to run back to that wrong 'safe haven'. But, fortunately, my resolve was sound and God helped me to cut it off and put it behind me forever.

When I was 19 years old and gave my life to the Lord, the spirit of python, like I said, worked tirelessly at trying to keep me bound in all of my dysfunction. That way he could hinder my faith and crush my vision so that he could control me and inundate me with a false sense of despair and powerlessness. By keeping me mentally locked in agreement with him he was able to interfere with my relationships, my finances, my jobs, people's perception of me, how they treated me, and so much more.

If the spirit of python succeeds at acquiring all this ground in one's mind and soul, he can constrict us indefinitely until the power of our Mighty God is grasped and loosed. But even if we somehow break free in our endeavors for Christ, all the devil has to try to do is cause us to stir up our carnal dust, re-establish a mental agreement rooted in our soul via old programming that has yet to be torn down, and he coils back around us for another season. And if the spirits have this much of a hold then it's as though we become their puppets and they can keep us in a place where we continue in endless cycles of defeat and our voices for God, muted. Where we are so oppressed that we don't have energy or desire to function or speak at all. Where we walk aimlessly in circles baffled at what is even going on with our lives.

The solution to keeping the spirit of python from suffocating or constricting the breath of life out of us is, first, to be sure we are hiding in the shadow of the Almighty. That really is the answer to every work of darkness against us. But another thing we should do is a self-examination of the soul. We must identify if there are, in fact, soul wounds or strongholds whereby self-pity or something else contrary to God is a definitive part of our programming. Like I said, self-pity comes from the dark kingdom. It has no place in the Kingdom of God. If we are citizens of the Most High God, then self-pity and every other negative condition does NOT belong in us.

Perhaps we were life-long victims, the ones who got the short end of the stick always. Maybe we were mistreated endlessly, were the object of scorn for so long. This will certainly prove to wire anyone to have a victim's mentality and always feel hurt and violated - even when no violations occur.

We have got to tear down every stronghold of pain. If you recognize this in yourself, seek Godly counsel and help to process things so that you can reject this from your life. It will require your taking the first steps of reaching out and reaching up to God. It will take prayer and perhaps deliverance and finally, it will take your deliberate rejection of this programming. The power is in you but it is up to you to utilize it. It is paramount otherwise the python will always know where you are and will continue to constrict you, suffocate you, and lure you into isolation and powerlessness. Again, we all have to come out of agreement with the idea we should feel sorry for ourselves and linger in sadness. In God's Kingdom, there is no hurt. And we were born into that very Kingdom! We were delivered from the kingdoms that hurt us. So, now we must let go of the mindset that we are still victims, still always being hurt by everyone. Because it is a lie! We do not have to embrace the ugliness of the other kingdoms.

True, we have feelings and are here in the natural kingdom where the dark kingdom reigns. Things do happen that do not feel good and hurt profusely at times. I am not suggesting that we are not to feel hurt. What I am saying is that we need to lose the victim's mentality and inclination to feel sorry for ourselves. We need to cut this off once and for all. It's a learning process, yes, where it might take a little while to practice walking out of it more and more, but that's okay. Just do it. One step at a time.

During our self-examination of the soul, we should also consider if there are roots of bitterness, hate, rejection, prideful self-preservation, fear, insecurity, inferiority, worry, unforgiveness, etc. If these are programs of the soul, the spirit of python will routinely create situations that will provoke those programs to run in us so that we will create all the dust he needs to discern us and attack. Remember, the spirit of python has no power over us unless we grant it. It is up to us to do whatever it takes to be deprogrammed from dark kingdom ways and thinking! And again, this may require reaching out for spiritual counseling. You'll need to confess, repent, and agree with someone that you are free from the false programs by the authority and power of Christ that is within you.

Whatever you do, do not undermine your need to deal with this aggressively. You might not want to turn to somebody. Perhaps you are so on guard that you refuse to trust anyone ever again. THIS IS PYTHON CONSTRICTING YOU! Don't keep listening. He doesn't want you to connect with another believer. Especially one who has overcome and knows who they are in Christ, who knows WHO CHRIST IS in them! There's so much power in uniting with the Body. That's the last thing the devil wants us doing. So NEVER, EVER, EVER stop trying to connect with solid believers. Be wise about it. Pray ahead of time asking the Lord whom HE says to reach out to. Asking who the right person is. Asking Him to show you who you can trust. If you are like I was, I resolved to trust no one. Honestly, that is okay. Don't put your trust in them. Put it in God! And let Him guide you to whomever - trusting that He'll be with you no matter what happens. If you are absolutely convinced there really is nobody you feel you can turn to, please write for prayer by emailing info@paulacross.com.

Next, repent of every wrong programming that makes you feel resistant towards uniting, renounce them. Ask God to forgive you and then believe that it really is under the Blood. Then pray that the enemy will not interfere with the right Godly friendship or elder in the church that you can confide in. Pray earnestly that the enemy will have no grounds to participate in your relationships or your encounters with people. And then finally, TRUST that God really is going to do what you have asked! Because He WILL!

Again, the spirit of python serves one purpose. You might think they hinder us just because they are evil and get their kicks that way. But the reality is their purpose is to promote their father to being god over all the earth. You and I are merely one of the billions he has to dominate in order to accomplish this. But you and I are being empowered by God to discontinue our covenants with the wrong kingdom and dethrone the false prophet. God is showing us the truth so that we can be free and can rise up in who we are in Christ and do the damage Satan is so desperately trying to keep us from causing! Python does not want us to receive the truth! The false prophet wants to keep us bound, keep us from walking in God's powerful presence, and keep our mouths shut. He is doing whatever he can to hinder us but we do not have to allow it any longer. To God be all the Glory.

Things To Consider

Has the false prophet worked effectively in your life at:

1. making you want to be alone
2. convincing you that you cannot trust anyone
3. keeping you distanced from other genuine believers
4. creating offenses, rejections and violations against you that continually separate you from others
5. programming your mind to be negative with the tendency to feeling bitter, self-pity, cheated, jealous, vengeful, or like everyone is against you
6. programming your soul to doubt that anyone (including God) truly loves and cares for real
7. programming your mind and soul to believe you have no value, that you are useless, hopeless, stupid or unintelligent, a failure, insignificant compared to everyone else, etc.
8. making you feel nothing will ever change; that God's promises will never make a difference in your life
9. making you feel suspicious and on guard all the time
10. making you wish you were never born

Chapter Review Checkpoints

1. Much like the natural python does, the spirit of python also constricts its victim. Whether we realize it's a spirit inflicting us or not, real physical symptoms occur such as:

    A. fatigue, lethargy, sluggishness, feeling paralyzed, overwhelmed, breathless

    B. foggy mindedness, indifference, apathy

    C. feelings of inadequacy, wanting to be alone, depression

    D. all of the above

2. The false prophet tries to program our minds early on to be negative and promotes our feelings of rejection, self-pity, lies that nobody loves us for 'real', etc. So long as these remain a part of our mental processes, the devil will maintain a powerful hold on our lives no matter how many years we are saved.
                      T or F

3. Through our relationship with Christ and by the power of the Blood, we can tear down such strongholds. And it is wise that we do this on our own.
                      T or F

4. Philippians 4:8 tells us that we are to ONLY think on things if they are of the following substance:

    A. hurtful and offensive, unjust and unfair

    B. true, just, pure, lovely, and of good report

    C. self-serving, self-preserving

    D. impure, unholy, the latest gossip

5. In order to better have his hand in our adult lives whether we get saved or not, (if he gets away with it) the false prophet must inundate us in our youth with things like

    A. pain, feeling rejected, and self-pity

    B. a negative perception of ourselves

    C. feelings of inferiority, inadequacy, self-loathing

    D. all of the above and so much more

6. The more the devil manipulates our minds in our youth, the bigger the wedge he hopes to put between us and our _____.

7. Another tactic the enemy will use is interfering in our lives in ways that make it seem like God doesn't care about us so that it is difficult for our soul to comprehend it even if our mind knows it.
                T or F

8. Bitterness, hate, rejection, pride, self-preservation, fear, insecurity, inferiority, worry, unforgiveness, self-pity, etc., may be programming operating in us at soul level and the false prophet will use these relentlessly to keep us under his

control. If we do not tear these roots out of our souls, we will continue

    A. to struggle getting into God's presence

    B. to be self-focused

    C. to be consumed with our problems

    D. to have difficulty focusing on the Word

    E. to have setbacks and misfortunes

    F. to have difficulty praising God

    G. to lack the peace and joy of the Lord

    H. to have difficulty praying

    I. to go in the same endless cycles of defeat

    J. all of the above and SO MUCH MORE

ANSWER KEY - CHAPTER IX
1-D, 2-T, 3-F, 4-B, 5-D, 6-God/Lord, 7-T, 8-J

Chapter Ten
Python & Our Finances

I was going on twenty-seven and was a single mother again but by now, with three children. And my livelihood? As it had always been... welfare. I had recently experienced discipline that brought me to a place of surrender and I was praying desperately that God would provide the way out of poverty. But I felt there was something invisible blocking me from finding it. There was a wall or barrier of sorts that was literally keeping me on welfare. I had felt it over the years every time I sought work. All I knew was every time I did try to get off the system the odds were against me and things never worked out. Literally. Even as I watched friends overcome who had no relationship with the Lord, who found the good jobs that I was equally qualified for, who broke free from welfare, I lagged behind for no sensible reason. Finally, it occurred to me that the way things had been going in my life were exactly the same as how they had gone for my mother all of her life. You see, I wasn't raised on welfare because she was lazy or unintelligent or lacked ambition. She was quite intelligent and ambitious. In fact, she had gone to several schools and received accreditation to be a secretary, a truck driver, to do upholstery restoration, real estate, do taxes, and finally, to be a nurses' aide. But try as she might to secure work in each of the fields, it wouldn't work out. And she was good at whatever she did. But it seemed some invisible force was working against her! So, she'd move on to something else thinking the next thing would be the right thing.

Well, I too, had gotten secretarial type credentials and when I saw that it wasn't paying off for me anddid not get me off of welfare, I did the same thing and went back for more education which did not work out either. The more I looked at the parallels between my mother's life and mine, the more peculiar it was. First, my mother was the first born, a daughter, born out of adultery (as her 19 year old married mother had had an affair). Next, she was put into a home as a newborn to be put up for adoption, but was retrieved and raised partially by her bitter mother, and partially by other family, foster care or girls' homes after being rescued from the grip of her mother's abuse at the tender age of six. The details of my life were different but revolved around the same elements as I, too, was the first born, a daughter, born out of adultery (as my 19 year old married mother had had an affair). And my mother, too, was persuaded to put me up for adoption. I, too, ended up in foster care and group homes in my youth due to extenuating circumstances. Then when I turned eighteen years old, I, too, bore a child out of wedlock, a daughter, and had been sent out of state to put her up for adoption but (while there) changed my mind and chose to keep and raise her. The cycle was continuing!

When I saw this, it really freaked me out! My life was a duplication of my mother's and grandmother's! And I said, "Lord, I do not want to continue in the cycle and I certainly do not want my daughter to fall into our same footsteps! I don't want her to go through similar situations in her childhood that we went through and I don't want her to think premarital sex is okay and have a child out of sin just to continue the cycle!"

Fortunately, I got to know the Lord and He told me when my daughter was small that the cycle stops with me through my life in Christ. He said my daughter is free from those generational curses, that she was the beginning of a new line - a heritage of blessings and grace in Christ. Subsequently, she didn't experience things in her youth that my mother and I had, she never went into foster care or group homes, and she got married at age 24. And I had said for years the icing on the cake in seeing the evidence that she is FREE from the cycle would be if her "legitimate" firstborn child was a SON. At one month shy of her 26th birthday, my daughter gave birth to their firstborn… a son. Incidentally, a baby name book I read years after my daughter was born told me her name meant "FREE". God had His mighty hand in my life working secretly in the midst of all the darkness that dominated me! Hallelujah!

At any rate, as that 19 year old, what I couldn't understand was how or why I was repeating the cycle because it was so strong in me as a child to want to grow up and do right. Plus, I was born again! I had God on my side! Yet, these weren't enough. And not because God is not strong enough. It was because, as God would soon reveal, there were forces of darkness built into me working from within as well externally in the circumstances of my life.

As I realized all of this, I was like, "Lord, what am I supposed to do? There's all this invisible power against me! You are a mighty God yet every time I take two steps forward I'm sent three steps back! If You are my God and more powerful, why is the darkness winning? And why am I trapped on welfare!"

This plagued my heart for several weeks in 1995 when one night I was watching Cornerstone (Christian) Television. They had a fund raiser going on.

It was the first time I ever saw such a thing. And this man, Dr. Mike Murdock, was speaking. He said, "There is a curse of poverty over your life!" and right away my spirit leapt. This was exactly what I had been feeling and it explained the dark forces I felt against me. This confirmed to me that there really were powers interfering with everything I put my hands to and that it wasn't coincidence nor was it my imagination. So, my antennas went straight up and I listened very carefully to what this man on Cornerstone had to say.

Suddenly, Dr. Murdock said, "God wants to break the back of poverty in your life!" and I got very excited because this was precisely what I was just praying about! I continued to listen and finally he said, "There's an anointing for one thousand dollar seeds. God wants you to let go of what is in your hands so that He can let go of what is in His." and I thought, "What? I don't have a thousand dollars! I live on $393 a month welfare with three kids. There's merely peanuts left after I pay the bills and buy diapers." But I thought further and said to myself, "Well, if he'll say I can give the thousand over the course of a year, I will do it." and just then, the very moment I said that to myself, Dr. Murdock said, "Don't let the devil steal this from you! You can do this over the next twelve months!" My stomach went into spasms. I began shaking. It was like I was having a one on one conversation with this man on my television. But another thought occurred to me. My new baby boy was a few months old now and I had been planning that by October which was a couple months away, I would have saved enough money left out of my monthly checks to get him a brand new walker. I really wanted to get a new one for him because the walkers my first two children had were used and this time I really wanted a new one. So, I said, "But Lord, I wanted to get the baby a walker in October," and He said, "You give me the seed and I'll give you the walker." I said okay.

I knew this was God. That God was using this man to show me how to overcome the curse that was on me. I didn't understand why or how until later, but I truthfully didn't care at the time. I was desperate and a peculiar answer was before me so I grabbed it with gusto. The only problem was I had no long distance and the phone number to the network was not toll free. So, I looked in my purse and found a one dollar bill, took it out, and decided if my neighbor's lights were still on who did have long distance (it was after 10:00 p.m.) I would knock on her door, offer her the dollar, and ask to use her phone. I went outside and looked anticipating her lights would be out because they usually were by then, but the entire apartment was lit up brighter than everyone else's! It felt as though it was an invitation to bother her (smile).

I have to tell you this was the most nerve racking phone call I think I have ever made. Not only was I in my neighbor's apartment (who was not a Christian and thought I was weird to begin with) calling a Christian television network to give away welfare money, but I was scared to death of committing to giving $1000 away. It may as well have been ten million. I was shaking, my stomach was in knots. But, I did it. I made the pledge.

God's voice became silent as the months began passing and I took whatever was left after the bills were paid and diapers were bought and sent it to Cornerstone Television. I had no set amount. I gave whatever was left.

Then October came and there was a knock on the front door. I opened it and there stood the children's father with a brand new….you guessed it - walker. I was stumped. Now you have to understand. The baby was five months old and his father had only seen him once since his birth and lived an hour away. We hadn't spoken but the one time as well. He was not even paying child support at that time. Yet, there he was. He had no idea what I had desired. It was strange….it was God. I asked, "What made you do this?

What prompted you to buy a walker?" and he said he just felt like it for no particular reason. I was so thankful. And I knew it was God stepping in to say, "Yes, Paula... This whole sowing a $1000 seed thing really IS of Me".

So, I continued sowing the seed. Even through Christmas. It was the one Christmas I spent absolutely nothing to purchase my children gifts because I wanted to be sure to keep giving all I had to Cornerstone Television. I wanted that seed 'in the soil'. I wanted the curse broken. I was eager to try to find work again and see that the devil couldn't interfere anymore.

Then January came and a good friend of mine suggested I try to sell water-based vacuums. I loved this machine and she had owned hers for years and swore by it. Having been a person who dealt with allergies to dust and such all my life, I was very much in favor of the mechanics of the product. Plus, my friend told me how cut out for it I was, that I would do so well selling them. And I believed her because I am a go getter and when I believe in something, I am determined to present a great case. Not only that, I was thinking about how I'd been sowing the seed into the soil for five months by then. Surely the forces against me would be smaller. Finally I could put my hand to something and see it work for a change.

Unfortunately, despite all the rave reviews I got for how great I was doing presenting these amazing cleaning machines, nobody would buy from me. Not a single machine. And I felt it. I felt the wall. It was all around me as thick as ever. And I walked away from it with my tail between my legs knowing that nothing at all had changed. The dark forces were still there.

In February, 1996 the monopoly over long distance telephone service providers had recently been abolished. All these new service providers jumped on the wagon and went into great competition. One particular service stood out among the rest with its awesome rates and offered great benefits to its sellers so I joined the team. I figured expensive cleaning systems were hard to sell, but everyone would want cheaper long distance service! But guess what….. I couldn't sign on a single customer no matter what I tried. It made no sense.

Suddenly, I became angry and felt like a fool. Come March when it was time to pay the bills and send whatever was left over to Cornerstone Television, I said no. Not anymore. I had been giving all I had and for what? To still be squashed every time I stepped up to bat. So, I decided my giving was done because it was nothing but a joke… on me.

Several weeks passed after refusing to send any more of the seed in and I was carrying a sort of bitterness over the situation. Then one night when it wasn't even on my mind, I crawled into bed to go to sleep and suddenly, in my mind's eye, I saw this person which I instantly understood to be me with this long, dark gray, rubbery thing coiled around her (the python). I referred to it as an Octopus even though there was no head or seven other legs. I have no idea why I called it that now that I look back since it did not look like an Octopus, but that's how I processed it, nonetheless Anyway, I didn't realize it was a vision from the Lord so I was like, "What the heck?" and right away I heard God say, "This is the curse of poverty in your life." I immediately sat straight up in bed and angrily cried, "Well, You said You were going to break its back!" and He said, "I did. But it's still hanging on and if you don't get the rest of the seed into the soil, it will remain a hindrance in your prosperity for the rest of your life."

This really shook me up so the next day I wrote out a check for whatever I had left and mailed it in. That evening, my one son who was in kindergarten, came in the door with his pile of school papers and the one jumped out at me. It was a science paper. The kids had cut out the pictures of seeds, the seeds being planted, and the seeds being watered, and then pasted them in the correct order. When I saw it, I heard the Holy Spirit say that I was back on track with getting the seed planted.

Then May came. I was going about my daily routine with the kids and out of nowhere something came into my spirit very strong. I felt the Lord say, "Take all the money in your bank account (before I paid all the bills) and add to it the amount that is coming in your next welfare check, and write the full amount out to Cornerstone Television." This was absurd, so I just ignored it. I chalked it up to my imagination. Surely God wasn't telling me to not pay my car insurance! Surely God wasn't telling me to give all my bill money away before I even got it!

The next day came and again, the idea came upon me quite strongly that I should do this, but again, I resisted. And then the next day it was there again. It just wouldn't let me go. It was on me so thick So, I prayed and asked God if this was really Him and there was great peace on me. He said to do it. So, I figured out what the combined amounts came to which was about $340, I wrote out the check and post-dated it, and I wrote a letter to Cornerstone Television explaining that they could NOT cash the check until the specified date because I hadn't yet received the funds and it wouldn't be in the bank for a couple weeks. And I mailed it.

Now nobody knew I had done this. Do you think I wanted to reveal how crazy I was just to hear people question and challenge me? So, I kept it to myself. I had no idea how I was going to pay the bills, but....

That week, I went to my friend Don's house. Don has cerebral palsy so he lives on a fixed income of social security. I stopped in to see him for whatever reason and as I was leaving, he lifted up his foot to me which had a $100 bill between his toes. He said, "God told me to give you $100." I was like, "No way!" because he didn't have much money himself! It was difficult to take it but I knew it was the Lord so I received it.

Within the next day or two, another friend of mine from church who had never been up to my new apartment in over a year randomly stopped in to see me. While visiting, she handed me a check and said, "Here, God told me to give you $100." And I was like, "Is this really happening?"

The next day or so I went to my mailbox and guess what was in it? Yes... another $100 check. This one was from the telecommunications company I tried to work for. I had forgotten that they said that even if you don't sell any long distance that you at least get $100 for trying or something like that. So there it was, that very week. I now had $300 back of the money I gave. But that wasn't it.

I was sitting on the living room floor with the kids playing when my best friend who lived across the parking lot poked her head in my door. She handed me two twenty dollar bills and said, "Happy Mother's Day, Paula"...

So there was my $340.00! All returned within a week! I was so excited. But that's not the end of the story. The Lord spoke to me one afternoon to pull out all my bank statements and add up all the money I had sent total to Cornerstone Television and when I did, I saw that it added up to $1005! I was astounded because I realized that that was why God told me to send all that I had - because He knew it was the full amount of the seed plus $5. And that evening when my son brought home his papers from school and I looked through them, I found a similar science paper to the one he'd done a month or so earlier. Only this time the first picture showed that the seed was already in the soil. The second picture showed somebody watering it. And the third picture showed the seed sprouting! The Lord spoke to me that my seed was in the soil and growing!!!

I was so excited I wrote another letter to Cornerstone Television and they ended up sending somebody to my home to interview and tape my story which they aired the following year during their fund raising weeks.

But while this was amazing, the fact was my seed was only just planted. It would take time to see what that seed would develop into. What would be the harvest? How would the back of poverty prove to be broken in my life?

Mind you, it was in May of 1996 that it was planted.... A lot was soon to transpire. So we'll jump two years forward to May 1998. By this time in my life, I hadn't qualified for cash assistance for a year and finally, no longer qualified for food stamps either! And we had our own medical insurance, not medical assistance. This was precisely when God spoke to me through Jentezen Franklin on Cornerstone Television one May afternoon (which happened to be my tenth birthday in the Lord and exactly two years since the seed was in the soil), "The back of poverty has been broken in your life! The python has been loosed!

The "python"? That's when I realized, that the rubbery thing was a python coiled around me in that vision... not an octopus!

At any rate, I was flabbergasted. It was finished! God was confirming that the curse was finally broken and I never received another government check or lived in government housing again! Of course, I would learn years later that there was more to the spirit of python than the curse of poverty over my life but that curse had to go first in order to recognize the others - and God took care of it.

There are several factors that led to my victory in this. First, I had to establish that I put my trust in God and not my welfare checks. God personally called me to give it away in order to define that my faith, my hope, wasn't in the welfare provision, but in Him. What I mean is because I had genuine needs and because those needs were strictly met via those welfare checks, they had become my source.

True, it 'may' have been a source God Himself provided for me but there's a fine line between relying on the source God provides and perceiving that source as THE source. God was giving me an opportunity to demonstrate what my confidence was in; Him or the welfare. So, He challenged me to trust Him when He told me HE would provide the walker and would work a miracle in my life whereby I would break free from my dependence on welfare. He asked me if I could let go of that which was what carried me and I said yes. By doing so, I demonstrated that I believed Him and was proclaiming that my dependence was in deed on Him; my hope and faith was in Him, not the welfare. God was providing me a way to come out of the curse of poverty and out of agreement with the false prophet by establishing that I believed and agreed with God.

    The second thing God taught me is the amazing power of seed faith giving. I came to understand that in order for increase to happen we have to apply the seed sowing principles because it's as real as how all other planted seeds grow and multiply.

    While I didn't get it at the time, I certainly understand now that since the spirit of python's agenda was to keep me down, he needed to always remain in control of my finances - or lack, thereof. Satan knows that a powerful way to constrict or squash someone's spirit is to keep them from succeeding at anything and especially keep them from earning their own way and in financial strife. If he could trap someone on welfare (or in poverty) and then lock them into false dependencies and thinking processes, they'd remain under his authority. And this would enable the enemy to continue stifling whoever they were supposed to be for God. They would never be able to develop their gifts and strengths in God if they remained bound to poverty due to a lack of understanding of truth and trust in the mighty God. They would additionally be hindered in their freedom to serve God due to a lack of funds or preoccupation with striving to keep the electricity from being shut off. It's quite simple, if the spirit of python can keep someone in poverty, will they reach their potential in Christ?

Of course, he doesn't manage to trap everyone on welfare or keep them in poverty but the same idea still applies to everyone who doesn't know the truth that God is a great provider for those who walk by faith, trust and obedience to Him. If Satan can keep somebody desperately preoccupied with earning "enough to survive" and keeping the utilities on, they won't be free to focus on serving God as much. If he can keep them stressed about finances and locked in the mind frame of lack so that they can't comprehend the truth of giving (because they are desperate to keep all they have for their survival) then they, too, are living according to the lies of dark government. God's truth and promises will not prevail for them; python will remain in authority over their finances.

While we are on the topic of giving, I want to share that I used to believe that tithing was a Biblical mandate wherein if you did not obey it and faithfully give ten percent of your gross earnings, then you were under a curse (according to Malachi 3). But this was all wrong. Search the scriptures and see that tithing as modern church culture presents it, that you are sinning if you do not, and you are under a curse, is not a Biblical doctrine. The Biblical implementation of tithing was food. In Leviticus 27, the mandate was given that one tenth, literally the tenth of the offspring born, whether good or bad, was to be given to the Levites, the servants of the priests who served to keep Israel cleansed from sin. Previously, Abraham gave a tenth of the spoils of war to Melchizedek. Meanwhile there were trades such as carpentry, fabric making, the selling of alcohol and many other livelihoods which were compensated for with money, yet there was never a single mention of a mandate to give a tenth of these earnings.

Later, in the New Testament, when Jesus reflected on tithing while rebuking the Pharisees (Matthew 23:23), He specifically named what was tithed on – and just like the Old Testament, it still had nothing to do with money or earnings of any sort. Further, Paul wrote two thirds of the New Testament and considering he addressed mostly gentile believers who never knew about Jewish customs such as tithing, every time he spoke to them concerning giving, he never once taught that this Jewish practice must be adopted by them. No, instead he said to give generously and cheerfully. And last, there is no mention of Jesus tithing on his carpenter wages or Peter on his fisherman income. Nothing. Are we to believe these could have been oversights if they were meant to be mandated practice in order to spare us from being under a curse?

Tithing certainly can be practiced out of one's own desire – and it's a great idea to choose to tithe off of our income if we so desire. But what the church teaches today is a manmade (or demon made) doctrine. What the Lord showed me was that because I believed in this false doctrine, I was unwittingly in agreement with the dark kingdom. God showed me this was a way for Python to continue to mess with my finances. Although I never had to get back on welfare again, there were peculiar setbacks and problems. Among various things the Lord showed me, the one thing Python had in me was I was ignorant to the truth of God – that God never said I'd be under a curse if I didn't give exactly ten percent of my gross earnings. Believing God said something He never said put me in alignment with the liar. And this was one huge reason Python had legal access to my resources, connections, blessings, and provision.

What I needed to do and did was renounce my agreement with the false doctrine and take authority in Christ over the minions assigned. They would have continued to operate against me had I not cast them out. In fact, what I precisely did was first repent that I didn't know the Word well enough to know any better. I repented for my ignorance which made me vulnerable to the lie I bought into because of my own negligence. After repenting, I renounced my previous agreeement. Then the Holy Spirit told me to take authority over the minions who had been working so diligently to keep the increase from coming and immediately I saw, in the spirit, a demon. He looked something like a genie the way he was sitting and floating over a giant sized version of my checkbook. He was sitting Indian-style with his arms crossed – hovering over my checkbook. Then I saw that there were many just like him over the other aspects of my life that had anything to do with financial increase. So, I took authority in the Name of Jesus Christ and commanded them to leave since the legal connection was abolished. Hallelujah.

    Last, I would like to discuss one more thing concerning giving. I've noticed over the decades that many Christians fuss about all the hype concerning seed faith giving saying it's wrong and nothing but a false prosperity doctrine. I won't sit here and suggest that it's all perfectly right and correct since I'm not God, not at all. A lot of it is NOT of God and we are to discern it and be careful. However, I would challenge everyone to be very cautious about conclusively speaking against as well. We are to practice discernment and we are not to be speaking on things which are not lovely or not of good report which means not grumbling about errors we do see. At any rate, I happened to have experienced that seed faith giving promoted in a right way by righteous ministry is real and God does use it to help people. It's merely a life principle. You plant, you reap. Not to mention the necessity of demonstrating your trust in God. And because we are called to be a blessing, to take care of the widows and orphans and to spread the gospel which costs money, it's our obligation to sow financial seeds "wisely" into God's

Kingdom in order to get His work done! We do need to investigate where we are sending our funds these days. But please do not despise every seed faith minister on the face of the planet just because some have perverted and/or abused it.

The griping... It is simply one of the wrong attitudes that the spirit of python has some Christian folks operating in in order to hold them back and keep them under. It really needs to stop so that we can all begin to walk in the full truth of God which does include... dare I say it? Prosperity.

Things To Consider

Just curious... Where does your hope and confidence truly lie? In your paycheck? In some other source? Or in God?

Chapter Review Chekpoints

1. Even though the Lord only ever commanded a tithe on the produce of the land in the Old Testament, while no other livelihood had such a command... And even though Paul never taught the Gentiles who were unfamiliar with Jewish customs about the tithe... And even though Jesus never tithed on his wages as a carpenter... It makes sense that the modern day church should teach that we are under a curse if we do not give ten percent of our income.
T or F

2. Paul's emphasis in the Bible concerning giving always pointed to

   A) Generosity
   B) Cheerfulness
   C) Ability
   D) All of the above

3. Is it likely that Jesus wants His children to trust Him enough to give Him whatever He asks of us at any given moment – be it 2%, 10%, 84% or 100%?

   Y or N

ANSWER KEY - CHAPTER X
1-F, 2-D, 3-Y

Chapter Eleven
Condemnation ~ One Slick Tool

"There is therefore now no condemnation to them which are in Christ Jesus, who walk not after the flesh, but after the Spirit." Romans 8:1 KJV.

There was a women's retreat I attended in the early 90's with the women from my church. While we were there, feeling heavily burdened, I was compelled to confess my battle with sexual sin. I cannot recall what led to this. The fact was I was one of the few women there who were unmarried. While I was in my mid-twenties, a mere baby in Christ, most of the women there were in their thirties and had been walking with the Lord for years. I admired them for so many reasons. But there I was carrying great shame because despite deciding not to fornicate and putting that lifestyle behind me, I slipped into to it several times - each time regretting it with every fiber of my being. I felt horrendously guilty and was so ashamed believing I would never be good enough in the eyes of the Lord.

Plagued by guilt and the need to unload, I went to the front of the room and revealed the truth, the whole truth, and nothing but the truth concerning my falling time and time again into sexual sin I forget what immediately transpired. Maybe I blanked out due to the stress of things? Perhaps. But what I recall later when we were able to spend time conversing with others after the session ended, a woman who I knew from my home church came to me and said, "Paula, I want you to know what I saw while you were up there sharing . You were surrounded in pure, bright white light, almost as though you were in a wedding gown or were an angel. You were just so pure white. You were so beautiful."

This touched me. I'm not sure I got the depths of what God intended that day but it lifted me a bit. I didn't fully understand yet I didn't feel as condemned as I had. Then another brilliant woman of God tenderly approached me and told me that there was no reason I should be walking in condemnation. I told her I understood but that I just felt horrible messing up over and over with something I know I'm not supposed to do! And that's when she said that this is where God's grace comes in and is sufficient. I wasn't hearing this because I continued to express how I just want to do right so that God could be proud of me, so that He would be pleased with me! And this is where she said something I will never forget. She put her hands on my shoulders, looked straight into my eyes, and said, "Paula, you can never do ANYTHING to make God proud of you!"

What? I was shocked! How cruel! But then she explained...

She said, "Paula, everything we do, including the good things, are like filthy rags (Isaiah 64:6). That's why He sent His Son to die for us and if we receive Him, that's Who God sees when He looks at us. He sees Jesus. It's Christ's righteousness that covers us and pleases God - not our good works."

I was beginning to understand but she had to elaborate. She impressed upon me that God understands that I'm prone to messing up and is why He had to die my death in the first place. And then she explained that God is pleased with me only because I chose Him, believe Him, and truly desire to honor and obey Him.

I did not know it at the time, but that night was huge in my history of deliverance from some of the grip of the python spirit. Up and until that day, I was under grave condemnation. And walking in self-condemnation is walking in agreement with dark kingdom principles, not

God's Kingdom truths. It is therefore yet another entry way the spirits can legally access us and influence our lives. I had accepted that Jesus paid my punishment but didn't grasp the full truth of His grace. I was bound up in self-condemnation and shame thinking I was less righteous because I wasn't walking in victory over my sexual sin yet! And when you think like this, you are in agreement with the liar of all liars who wants to keep you bound up even if you are Blood bought and REDEEMED. He is free to pound this into our spirits daily if we'll listen and it'll simply weigh us down and hinder our self-confidence, our freedom to love and live life to the fullest in Christ. It gives him the ability to constrict us all the more!

This is what must be grasped! If we believe the devil every time he tells us we are losers because we fall, we will live life defeated. The truth is that there really is no condemnation for those who are in Christ Jesus. Yes, I did fall at times, but I wasn't choosing to go back to that lifestyle. I did not practice fornication as a way of living. If I had decided to make it my lifestyle again, I would have been rejecting Christ. But as it was, it was a major shortcoming that I had trouble with from time to time that I was too weak to resist and I felt like a complete failure. I hated it! I felt God was forever disappointed in me. I could just imagine Him shaking His head at me saying, "For crying out loud, she knows better than to do this!" That is until God showed me that there IS NO RIGHTEOUSNESS IN ME outside of Christ! That I was a failure apart from Him and His power in me which would be my way to victory - and that my obedience was never impressive because it would be by His power I obey anyway! My submission and yielding - but HIS POWER. I learned that what mattered to God was that it was my heart that desperately wanted to obey and that was why His Blood covered me. That's why He said I was pure white. He was telling me that because my heart genuinely rejected the sin and embraced God, that Jesus was my covering so that when He looked upon me, He only saw the pure, HOLY, righteousness of Jesus Christ! And it made me beautiful!

As much as I thought I got it that night, something still wasn't clicking in me because several weeks later the Lord addressed me again on the same matter. I still felt some shame. Not necessarily due to my propensity to fail but because of my entire past and childhood where I felt so small, squashed and inferior.

Many of us ladies from church drove to another city where a prophetess was coming to speak. On the van ride there something peculiar happened that sent me into the remembrance of what had happened months earlier. There was an older woman sitting in the seat in front of me and she turned around and said to me out of nowhere, "You know, I have to tell you.... I don't know what it is about you but when I look at you I can't help thinking you are so beautiful!"

What in the world was going on? I knew I wasn't ugly but I certainly wasn't beautiful. Especially that night! I was in the dumps, left my hair drabby and didn't bother to put any make-up on. I was not looking my best to say the least. So, what was this all about? All I knew was this was the second time in weeks I heard such a peculiar comment.

Anyway, I was kind of ignorant concerning prophetic ministry but it didn't matter. While there, the lady prophet (who I had never seen before) called me up to the front. I was nervous but I wasn't expecting much. She'd called others up and nothing all that profound was being said so... Whatever... But when I got before her, she powerfully placed her hand on the back of my neck and passionately cried, "This tension be gone!"

This astounded me because I had been having issues with my neck curvature due to tension and had been to the chiropractor over it for a few years. So, her going right to the area was my alert that God was indeed on the scene and she had my full attention. (By the way, I learned down the road that the enemy tries to cripple our bodies by inundating us with anxiety and tension. She (the Lord) was binding the spirits of python who were working against me in that fashion - who were causing the curvature of my neck to go in the opposite direction! And it worked.)

Anyway, immediately following her grabbing my neck and saying that, she grabbed my chin and pushed my head up a bit commanding, "You hold your head up high! You are the apple of my eye! Do not be ashamed, you keep your chin up! I was there with you in second grade when you felt rejected (I had just returned home from foster care that year) But I am for you. You are beautiful; hold your head high... you are the apple of my eye."

Now I understood completely. God was reaching down and addressing my shame once and for all. He had dispelled some of the self-condemnation a few weeks prior making me see that I couldn't do a thing to impress Him. But now He was adding that even though I'm nothing apart from Him, He adores me. He thinks I'm beautiful because my heart was pure and I longed to obey Him. He thinks of me as the apple of His eye!

Can you imagine how ticked off the false prophet was the moment God soared down from Heaven, pierced through the darkness that surrounded me and told me the TRUTH!?!? Hallelujah!

The next morning I was in our Sunday morning church service and the worship team began to play the very first song... "We are Your treasured possession and the apple of Your eye..." Whew! Could God make it any more obvious? He loved me! He always confirms what He says through other sources.

If you have lived a life of shame, feeling weighed down and defeated just for 'being you' or because you are always messing up, reject this lie right now. I know, I know... It's not easy to comprehend that you are valuable and adored if you were never treated that way. But it's the TRUTH! Start treating yourself according to it. Forgive those who failed you and come into the truth! And forgive yourself for not being something other than what you are! You are exactly the way God wants you to be!

If this is a long-term issue for you...where you hate yourself for being such a failure, where you are so ashamed and small, I want you to look to God right now and ask Him to help you comprehend this once and for all. If you truly want to live for Jesus and received His gift of salvation, you are completely righteous! God is looking upon you right now and sees nothing but the glow of Christ all about you. You are fantastically beautiful! Reject the shame. Come out of agreement with the liar! Come out of agreement with the government of darkness! You must reject these lies if you want his power in this area to cease! Lift your head up and receive God's touch right now - right where you are. Don't allow the spirit of python to keep you locked in the lie and programming of self-condemnation another minute. Look up and say, "Father, I am the apple of Your eye! You adore me!" and repeat it the rest of the day and the rest of your life!

Things To Consider

Are you ashamed, heavy ladened, weighed down with guilt? If yes, should you be?

Chapter Review Checkpoints

1. If you feel you will never be good enough on your own, you should praise God and not feel ashamed or guilty at all! Because the truth is we all fall short and desperately need God's help to walk right!
                          T or F

2. When we receive Christ as Lord and Savior, we are to pursue God's righteous ways by following His precepts and Ten Commandments to the best of our ability. But sometimes we fall. When we do, we should

    A. beat ourselves up and be ashamed of ourselves

    B. go to confession

    C. do nothing because it's covered by the Blood

    D. repent and quickly turn back - thanking God for His precious mercy and forgiveness

3. The false prophet wants us to feel guilt ridden for not being perfect because that means we haven't embraced

    A. truth

    B. grace

    C. the Cross

    D. all of the above

4. If you truly desire to obey God with all of your heart (even if you fail at times), this is pleasing to the Lord.
T or F

5. If you are born again and feel guilt, shame, or condemnation even after genuinely repenting from sin and turning from it, then you

    A. are in agreement with the dark kingdom

    B. are just going through normal grieving

    C. are not walking in the truth of grace which reduces
the value of the death Christ died for you

    D. A and C

ANSWER KEY - CHAPTER XI
1-B, 2-D, 3-T, 4-T, 5-D

Chapter Twelve
Praise Power & Position

Another key to dethroning the false prophet concerns the python's need to keep us from realizing God's love, power, and the authority we have through Christ. I'm going to jump back to a remarkable situation that took place in my life in 1992. I had been pursuing God passionately during this season and His love began to permeate my soul. The Holy Spirit began giving me visions and speaking directly to me concerning the situations at hand. He brought me to a place of awe at how personally interested in 'me' He was. And He set out to teach me something extraordinary.

I had been attending my new church for more than a year at that time and was very involved. In fact, the church and all the wonderful people became my new family. Something like home group or picnics were going on pretty routinely so it would be peculiar if one of us disappeared for awhile. Yet, that's what had happened to me and it appeared to go completely unnoticed. My depression welled up to where I was physically immobile. My daughter was five now, and the baby, two. A few weeks had gone by where I barely got out of bed let alone out of the house or to church or anything. If we desperately needed groceries I would drag myself to get them and then shut back down. One day my two year old stood at my bedside saying, "Mommy, I need a dwink." I lay there feeling completely incapable of going downstairs to get him a simple glass of water! He may as well have been asking me to do back flips. That's how incapacitated I was.

Throughout those few weeks I desperately prayed over and over, "Please send somebody to help me, Lord, please send somebody to help me". I didn't want to call anyone. I was too weak and ashamed. Besides, when I got pressed down like that, I honestly didn't want to talk to anyone. I'd shrink down to nothing and reaching out is the last thing I would do for myself. But I thought if God would send the right person who wouldn't look down on me, who would know what to do, then all would be well. But nobody came. Even my regular friends were somehow not calling to get together which was very unusual. Yet, I kept praying daily for God to send someone.

Python had me bound quite well. My mind was shot. My ambitions were squashed. I felt alone. I was powerless to stand and do the simplest things of life. My apartment was a wreck. What kind of a loser was I? How would I ever give my children a good life? And welfare..... I was on welfare just as my pastor feared I would be six years earlier when I found out I was pregnant out of wedlock. I was a menace to society. A strain. I wasn't an asset. I had nothing to offer the world to make it a better place. I took from the world and gave nothing back. I brought children into the world to be fatherless.... And then I would cause my child to have to beg me for water. I hated myself desperately.

But the Living God was "for" me and He saw my distress and would rescue me!

After three weeks passed and I saw no sign of deliverance, I lay awake one night downstairs on the couch listening to Christian teaching tapes which I had forced myself to turn on. The tape I was listening to, by Mahesh Chavda, was teaching on the authority of the Holy Spirit. I lay there listening to the Word but powerless until he said, "You have the authority of Christ in you" and suddenly I don't even remember the cassette continuing because an invisible, holy power fell on me. All at once I went from feeling strapped down, lifeless, trapped and empty to a state of complete exhilaration! Intense electrical energy was in me and I heard the Holy Spirit say "You don't need somebody to come to you to help you. Christ Who lives in you is All Authority! The answer to your problem is in you! Now rise up and take authority!"

    I did not understand what was going on but it didn't matter because I was excited and feeling powerfully charged so I jumped up and began praising God. I mean I PRAISED God! I was on fire and overwhelmed with joy. The holy power consumed me and filled me with a glorious passion for the wonder of God! I danced and I proclaimed the glory of God! I praised Him with all that was within me. And then it came out of my mouth as I looked at my hands, "These are HOLY HANDS! This is HOLY GROUND! Nothing has authority here but GOD!" and I continued to exalt Him with all that was within me. And I took authority, in the Name of Jesus, over my life and circumstances.

    After some time of this the Lord spoke to me to go upstairs and pray over my daughter. She had been struggling with some things and I had basically thrown my arms up in the air in defeat. There was nothing I could do to remedy the issues.. So I obeyed the leading of God and went into her bedroom, radiating in the light of God, full of the Holy Spirit. I tiptoed over to her bed and praised God passionately under my breath. I remember being in such awe, declaring that He was indeed the Most High God. After a while of this something strange happened. Mind you, I was praising and praying at a very low whisper, basically under my breath, when suddenly I went from speaking in English to some unknown language. It took me by great surprise because I had never spoken in tongues before. Yet there I was, uttering unknown words, going back and forth between English and this tongue, from praising Him Who had all authority, to praying for His hand to move on our behalf. This transpired for several minutes and then something even more peculiar happened. As I stood there, with my arms raised praising Him, going from English to tongues, suddenly out of my mouth I looked up to Heaven, raised my right hand back up, and cried, "Father, pour out Your power like a lightning bolt!" At that very instant, from two doors down the hall where my two year old was soundly sleeping, I heard him defiantly shout, "NO!"

This stopped me in my tracks. I became very still. What had just happened? My son doesn't talk in his sleep! I had the clear understanding that this reflected something supernatural; something beyond the natural realm. No, I did not feel my son was possessed or anything, but I did feel his voice was used to let me hear a glimpse of what was going on around me in the spirit realm.

This startled me and brought me to silence but after only a moment, the Lord spoke to me very vividly, "Keep praising Me", and so I did. I resumed. I dove right back into the powerful presence that enveloped me and I continued as I had been, praising and praying the might of God. After several minutes of this, and again, going from English to tongues, I found myself once again throwing my arm up to Heaven as though there was a sword in my hand and shouting under my breath, "Father, pour out Your power like a lightning bolt!" and instantly my two year old son defiantly cried from his bedroom, "I DON'T WANT TO!"

Once again I was stifled. I knew that I knew that I knew something was going on there. It made no sense to me at all yet, it was powerful and such reverence fell on me to be witnessing something so holy take place right before my eyes, even though I had no idea what it was. But like before, after standing there for a moment, the Lord spoke to me and said, "Keep praising Me."

I resumed once again and kept going until I heard the voice of God say to me, "Peace. Go to bed."

The next day I was alive again. I had strength and ambition. I began cleaning my apartment and taking deep breaths of freedom. But all through the day I remembered what had happened through the night and out of reverence decided I wouldn't even ask God. He knew what had happened. If He wanted me to know more, He'd tell me.

Later that evening, low and behold, for the first time in weeks, one of my best friends called me. At first I said nothing about what had happened. To be honest I didn't want it to be misconstrued, for her to think I was crazy, or worse, to think my son was demonized. But after a while I began to share the story and when I told her how both times I prayed, "Father, pour out Your power like a lightning bolt" my son shouted first 'no' and then 'I don't want to', she began crying. I asked her what was wrong and she said, "Paula, when You told God to pour out His power He said to the devil, 'GET OUT!' and the devil said no. So He told you to keep praising Him and later, when you said it again, God said, "I SAID GET OUT!" and the devil continued to resist saying he didn't want to. So God told you to keep praising Him because you were releasing His power which was forcefully chasing the enemy out of your home." ~Wow. God is so good. I had no idea. With that the Lord elaborated by speaking to my spirit that what was wrong with me for those three weeks was called "oppression"- not so much of a "depression". The enemy was literally in my home pressing down on me, suffocating me. Now this was all God enabled me to see at that time. It wouldn't be until many years down the road that I would understand that this was one of the works of python against me and how it was that these devils were able to get away with it in the first place since I was redeemed. The fact was I had been pursuing all truth like never before and began to grow as a child of holiness and the enemy had to squash me.

But wait a minute. The Bible teaches that the serpent's venom is powerless against children of God. Why was it not powerless against me?

This was a perfect example of submitting to Satan's government. Remember, if we agree with any spirit, we are granting that spirit rights and give it permission to be a part of our lives. And just what rights had I unwittingly granted? If you recall, I said I hated myself. This is NOT of God's Kingdom! Because of my history, the hurts, the confusion, my failures, all of it, I grew up hating myself and went into covenant with a spirit of self-loathing. When I began attending the new church and seeing the love of God, the enemy had to defuse it. He couldn't allow the truth of love to get a hold of and change me because that particular enemy would lose its authority in my life. Because if I would come to understand that I really am loved, I would reject the lie that I am a big fat, worthless piece of nothing. So, not-so-great situations began happening with the most loving people I'd ever known which provoked my feelings of smallness and rejection. Python strategically orchestrated offenses and hurts that would derail me and cause me to agree with his suggestion that nobody cared about me or whatever. And then I'd resort to my wrong programming and shrink away from people - coming into even deeper agreement again with dark kingdom principles. I'd begin meditating on how horrible I was and how badly I hated myself - giving him even MORE legal ground to suck the breath of life out of me! Satan is a master at using the snowball strategy of starting small and thrusting us deeper and deeper into darkness. And as I would go into the familiar mode he'd taken me into so many times before in my life, it would empower the spirit to oppress me to where I would be physically immobile and dysfunctional!

Understand that Python seriously needed to do this because I was getting closer to God and the closer to God you get, the more powerful you become. And the more powerful you become, the more ground he loses and the greater the threat you are to his kingdom!

People might argue that negative thinking alone is powerful and can be the reason for the depression and physical depletion I endured. In fact, even the Bible says laughter is good medicine suggesting negative feelings would be bad for the body. While I'm not an expert in the field, I have heard how poor thinking reduces certain hormone levels like serotonin causing things such as depression. So, I'll be the first to admit my negative thinking patterns were a huge enemy of mine in and of themselves. As a matter of fact, a couple years later I started getting therapy and came to recognize the relationship between negative thinking and depression.

But while this was all true, the Lord didn't stage that spiritual battle where my son shouted defiantly from two bedrooms away for my entertainment. He was teaching me something very important. God was allowing me to witness a bit of what was going on supernaturally. Sure, my negative thinking helped reduce my serotonin levels so maybe that's why it was so difficult to go get my two year old his drink. But the rest of the story undeniably includes the fact that there were dark entities at work in my midst driving me down. Otherwise, what was the point of God showing up and leading me in praise, worship… and warfare? I was there. I was the one physically bound and suddenly empowered by an invisible electricity that felt beautiful and glorious. I was the one who heard within my depths the Lord speak to me about the authority of Christ that was in me. I was the one led to praise and pray having no clue at the time that scriptures tell us that there is power in praising God. This was why in the story with Paul and Silas being thrown into prison after casting the python spirit out of the girl, God broke them free miraculously! There truly is GREAT power in praise and worship! I experienced it firsthand! I was the one being delivered from heavy darkness. I was the one in chains who praised the Lord at His leading and felt them bust right off of me!

There was no doubt in my mind that God showed up for me that night and taught me firsthand about the power of praise as well as the reality that the devil really is at work against us. But something absolutely wonderful happened about a month or two later while reading the Psalms that, putting it simply, put the icing on the cake.

Psalm 18 NIV

1 I love you, O LORD, my strength.
2 The LORD is my rock, my fortress and my deliverer;
my God is my rock, in whom I take refuge.
He is my shield and the horn of my salvation, my stronghold.
3 **I call to the LORD, who is worthy of praise**,
and I am saved from my enemies.
4 **The cords of death entangled me**;
the torrents of destruction overwhelmed me.
5 **The cords of the grave coiled around me**;
the snares of death confronted me.
6 **In my distress I called to the LORD**;
I cried to my God for help.
From his temple he heard my voice;
my cry came before him, into his ears.
7 The earth trembled and quaked,
and the foundations of the mountains shook;
they trembled because he was angry.
8 **Smoke rose from his nostrils**;
consuming fire came from his mouth,
burning coals blazed out of it.
9 He parted the heavens and came down;
dark clouds were under his feet.

10 He mounted the cherubim and flew;
he soared on the wings of the wind.
11 He made darkness his covering, his canopy around him—
the dark rain clouds of the sky.
12 Out of the brightness of his presence clouds advanced,
with hailstones **and bolts of lightning.**
13 The LORD thundered from heaven;
the voice of the Most High resounded.
14 He shot his arrows and scattered the enemies ,
great bolts of lightning and routed them.
15 The valleys of the sea were exposed
and the foundations of the earth laid bare
at your rebuke, O LORD,
at the blast of breath from your nostrils.
**16 He reached down from on high and took hold of me;
he drew me out of deep waters.
17 He rescued me from my powerful enemy,
from my foes, who were too strong for me.**

    Bolts of lightning? God led me to scripture that was exactly what I had lived even to the routing of my enemies with bolts of lightning! I had wondered what compelled me that night to cry, "Father, pour out Your power like a lightning bolt!" Twice, no less! It was the Lord speaking His words through my mouth. But do you want to know the most wonderful part about discovering this Psalm? Psalm 18:7 where it reveals the heart of God. See, up until reading this I saw the deliverance as a great thing that God showed up. But it was more, "Well, that's what a mighty God does. He kicks butt." But now I saw the condition of His heart in it. God wanted me to know He was furious about my distress at the hand of evil! The fact of the matter was He didn't just casually step on the scene to help because he had some extra time on His hands. No! Rather, He was livid!

He was angry! Smoke rose from his nostrils! He was furious with the spirit of python and he routed the oppressors out of my midst with violent force! My God was passionately rescuing me! And He wanted me to KNOW it!

But do you see what the false prophet was trying to do at this time in my life when I was getting to know God in a very real and tangible way? He knew God was passionate for me. And he saw me discovering the goodness and love of God through the church I was involved in. So, he had to counter-attack and isolate me. He had to cause me to feel alone and dejected. He had to work earnestly at distancing me from the church and truth by causing offenses and reminding me how inferior he'd always said I was.

This is what the spirit of python works most aggressively at doing to believers. If he can isolate us or squash our spirits, we become useless. So we must become wise to this and ward off and resist every last form of offense and ill feelings we get towards other believers and ourselves! We must resist the temptation to distance ourselves from other believers no matter what. Every bit of it is a plot to shut us down so that God cannot flow in our midst as freely and powerfully as He longs to. Causing us to be irked with one another even to the slightest degree is one of the devil's policies. It's of his kingdom. I don't care what the offense or violation is. It's implemented by the government of Satan and we cannot allow these things to control us. We must realize it's the devil, the powers and principalities of the air and not the people! We cannot let the devil get away with this any longer! Serious times are coming. We don't have time to be oppressed and isolated anymore. We must join together in harmony, love, self-control, kindness, joy, unity, and long suffering. Sound familiar? We must come to know the truth of who we are in Christ, the authority we have in Him, resist the liar, and rise up in power as one, unified body.

We must know who we are! We must know that God is for us and that His AUTHORITY is ALL POWERFUL and lives within us! And we must understand that as we grasp these truths and we praise Him with all our hearts, His glory will rise up in us and we will be victorious!

Things To Consider

Remember the importance of praising God. No matter what situation you are in, it releases the power and authority of Christ to overcome darkness.

~ If you find it difficult to praise God in any given situation, do it anyway! It's called a sacrifice of praise. Do not allow the enemy to ever shut your mouth and squash your heart of praise for the Lord! If you can't do it, the enemy has a hold on you. RESIST it, in the Name of Christ! Do not be defeated by evil. Praise God CONTINUALLY and in ALL things!

Chapter Review Checkpoints

1. When we begin growing in the Lord, getting close to other believers and God in a real and tangible way, the false prophet may try to interfere with those relationships by provoking rejection, offenses, and disunity.
T or F

2. God is infuriated when the enemy oppresses His children.

T or F

3. It is sometimes difficult to praise the Lord - especially if we are going through something dreadfully painful. But if we will offer up sacrificial praise even when we don't feel like it, we will be loosing God's

   A. power

   B. authority

   C. manifest presence

   D. all of the above

4. If we are struggling to praise God, this is an indication that the enemy has a hold on us and we should resist his resistance.

T or F

5. A powerful way to rise up in the authority of Christ, to loose His power against our foes, is to simply magnify, exalt, and praise God with all our hearts.

T or F

ANSWER KEY - CHAPTER XII
1-T, 2-T, 3-D, 4-T, 5-T

Chapter Thirteen
Victory Nay Embraced

"I know that nothing good lives in me, that is, in my sinful nature. For I have the desire to do what is good, but I cannot carry it out. For what I do is not the good I want to do; no, the evil I do not want to do—this I keep on doing. Now if I do what I do not want to do, it is no longer I who does it, but it is sin living in me that does it… What a wretched man I am…" Romans 7:18-20 & 24 NIV.

This passage continues on to explain that through Christ we are no longer enslaved to the nature of sin. But it seems we just don't get this. For some of us, it is our propensity as believers to get stuck at "What a wretched man I am" and fail to embrace the victory spoken of in both the preceding and proceeding chapters. We think, "Well, I can never be perfect as a human. It's my nature to sin even though I don't want to. That's why Christ died for me."

This seems all well and good but it shows that the victory made available to us is not embraced. And it's not right. This is a false way of thinking that we certainly can assume comes straight from the author of falsities! This line of thinking stops extremely short of the full truth that says we literally are victors in Christ. That we are no longer slaves or bound to our old ways - including our propensity to sin. Because, "We know that our old sinful selves were crucified with Christ so that sin might lose its power in our lives. We are no longer slaves to sin. For when we died with Christ we were set free from the power of sin." Romans 6:6-7 NLT.

Unfortunately, this is an aspect of truth the false prophet works tirelessly to hide from believers. It's the spirit of python who promotes this fatalistic perspective.

It's a twisted programming that says, "I will never stop sinning as long as I'm still on earth because it's human nature!" Meanwhile, we've received power from on High to override our human nature but we're oblivious. So many of us fail to realize that we've been infilled with a power from God that says we no longer have to remain wretched. We are clueless as to the full nature of our new identity and seem to prefer remaining as failures! The result is our walk with God is dreadfully stifled! I wonder how much glory is lost to God by our half-baked Christendom.

It's sad to say but I think more of the Body of Christ is stuck in this rut than not. We embrace salvation but fail to realize the full victory availed to us. This certainly explains our casual response to the sins we undermine which trap us in living powerless, non Christ-like lives. We go through our days disturbed with sinners locked in their morbid lifestyles but excuse our own subtle iniquity which grieves our precious Lord just the same - if not more. For example, if a friend told us they genuinely intended to murder their pesky neighbor, alarms would go off! Our response would be aggressive, "What! No! You can't do that! Are you crazy???" Yet, if we witnessed our friend responding to the pesky neighbor in a way that's not motivated by love, perhaps by deliberately parking in an area they dispute over, for example, our response is hardly comparable. Yes, the intensity of murder far outweighs the impact of pinching somebody with our pride so we certainly won't respond as aggressively. But while murder is horrid, isn't it true that God opposes the proud? Is that not equally dangerous? Why are we appalled by the big stuff but shrug off the 'little' things as though it's no big deal to God? Of course, some of us might actually attempt to do a right thing and encourage our friend to forgive or suggest solutions to a loving resolve, etc. But why are we not concerned about the damage a simple thing like pride causes? Why do we not care that God made a point to declare His opposition to the proud!

We could write an entire book listing examples of sinful behaviors that our Christian culture nowadays is typically passive about compared to ones we are not. Such as homosexuality. For the majority of believers, we are still resolved that this lifestyle is wrong (but even that seems to be going out the window!). The same goes for drug usage and drunkenness. We are solid in our Christian perspective that such things are blatantly contrary to the ways of God. Yet, if any of us are over eaters, are materialistic, tend to gossip or regularly speak on things which are not lovely or of good report, make decisions out of fear or carnal logic rather than by faith, or perhaps love the world just a bit more than we ought... Or if we tend to worry, are evasive, controlling, lazy or manipulative, walk in pride or selfish ambition or lack self-control... We accept these as normal shortcomings and let them slide because, after all, we're only human.

These behaviors are plainly addressed in scripture yet we are becoming profusely apathetic to the truth of them - even after years of claiming to belong to Christ! I think a huge part of why the body at large does this is because we are trapped in an evil induced thinking that says we're prone to sin.

But it's WRONG! This type of thinking is a snare to our relationship with God and it's an insult to grace! It's as much from the pits of hell as believing gay marriage or abortion is acceptable! The spirit of python avidly works to keep us from coming into the complete understanding of the Gospel which includes the mandate to walk in righteousness and into the full victory availed to us by our precious Mighty King Who was crushed for our sakes!!! We must not listen to the liar and live these feeble lives where we say, "But, I am not a drunk, a thief, liar, drug addict, prostitute or pimp. I don't cheat on my spouse or even look at the opposite sex or pornography, I give my money to God, I'm a good Samaritan who always helps out when I can, I don't cuss, I don't watch R rated movies, I forgive others, I read my Bible and go to church". Sure, this shows we fear and love God plenty since we honor Him in practicing these ways. But our honor must not stop there! Our complete honor and love for God means we revere ALL of God's teachings and never undermine things He says are wrong! If God says lacking self-control is not good, for example, then how often is it okay to let it slide! NONE! Again, how much slippage in this area is acceptable? ZERO! We are so quick to regret if we burst out into an uncontrollable rage because it's obviously wrong yet we completely ignore the conviction of the Holy Spirit if we, say, murmur and complain??? Shouldn't we feel equally repentant in every area that we fall??? Do we not understand that ALL willful sin comes between us and our God? Not that we should beat ourselves up if we fail when we really are trying to do right because this is where grace covers us. But the rest of the truth of grace is we are no longer enslaved to ANY sin and we seem like we just don't care. Meanwhile, we should be embracing the power that was born into us, nurturing it with faith, and growing it up so that sin really does lose every hold on us.

"So you also should consider yourselves to be dead to the power of sin and alive to God through Christ Jesus. Do not let sin control the way you live; do not give in to sinful desires. Do not let any part of your body become an instrument of evil to serve sin. Instead, give yourselves completely to God, for you were dead, but now you have new life." Romans 6:11-13 NLT.

It is so interesting that in Romans 6:7 Paul says, "For when we died with Christ we were set free from the power of sin" and then four verses later he says, "So you also should CONSIDER yourselves to be dead to the power of sin..." Consider? In verse seven Paul is establishing that the power of sin which was born into us by human nature is, in fact, now powerless against the believer. Yet, in verse eleven, he exhorts us to choose to embrace this reality and make it our own. In other words, it became possible that sin no longer had to have power but still does unless we purposefully embrace, "Hey, I don't HAVE to be enslaved anymore! And by the power of Christ Who is in me Who broke the power of sin off of me, I won't be!" We have to embrace and possess this truth on purpose!

Isn't it odd that we are so complacent concerning holy living in ALL areas when 1 John 2:4-6 boldly conveys, "The man who says, 'I know him,' but does not do (all of) what he commands is a liar, and the truth is not in him. But if anyone obeys (all of) his word, God's love is truly made complete in him. This is how we know we are in him: Whoever claims to live in him must walk as Jesus did."

Continuing in 1 John 2, verses 15 and 16 declare, "Do not love the world or anything in the world. If anyone loves the world, the love of the Father is not in him. For everything in the world—the cravings of sinful man, the lust of his eyes and the boasting of what he has and does—comes not from the Father but from the world."

My brothers and sisters, isn't it time we truly comprehend that...

"By his divine power, God has given us everything we need for living a godly life. We have received all of this by coming to know him, the one who called us to himself by means of his marvelous glory and excellence. And because of his glory and excellence, he has given us great and precious promises. These are the promises that enable you to share his divine nature and escape the world's corruption caused by human desires. In view of all this, make every effort to respond to God's promises. Supplement your faith with a generous provision of moral excellence, and moral excellence with knowledge, and knowledge with self-control, and self-control with patient endurance, and patient endurance with godliness, and godliness with brotherly affection, and brotherly affection with love for everyone." 2 Peter 1:3-7 NLT.

"For if you possess these qualities in increasing measure, they will keep you from being ineffective and unproductive in your knowledge of our Lord Jesus Christ." 2 Peter 1:8 NIV.

The deliverance from sin is established as I've previously shared but then the mandate to live holy is made most evident in Romans 6:19 NLT: "...Previously, you let yourselves be slaves to impurity and lawlessness, which led ever deeper into sin. Now you must give yourselves to be slaves to righteous living so that you will become holy."

Even more so in James 4:4-10 NLT: "You adulterers! Don't you realize that friendship with the world makes you an enemy of God? I say it again: If you want to be a friend of the world, you make yourself an enemy of God. What do you think the Scriptures mean when they say that the spirit God has placed within us is filled with envy? But he gives us even more grace to stand against such evil desires. As the Scriptures say, 'God opposes the proud but favors the humble.' So humble yourselves before God. Resist the devil, and he will flee from you. Come close to God, and God will come close to you. Wash your hands, you sinners; purify your hearts, for your loyalty is divided between God and the world. Let there be tears for what you have done. Let there be sorrow and deep grief. Let there be sadness instead of laughter, and gloom instead of joy. Humble yourselves before the Lord, and he will lift you up in honor."

Yes, clearly.... We are commanded to walk uprightly and more, to not brush it off when we fail to! There should be nothing casual about our walk with the Lord. We are to take up our cross and follow Him. Living 'in' Christ is dying to self. We are to not conform to the ways, the foolishness, the perversions, the apathy, and the debauchery of the world! We are to keep our eyes and ears from evil so that they are not polluted. We are to be lights of love, peace, joy, and kindness in a dark and corrupt world. We are to be the head and not the tail (leaders of righteousness, not followers of foolishness). We are to be representatives of all of His truths! We are representatives of Christ! It is time to repent of our complacency in what it TRULY means to be Christians!

Jesus tells us the Ten Commandments can be summed up into two - love the Lord our God with all our hearts, mind, and strength; and love our neighbors as ourselves. When we do these, when we truly love God first with all our hearts and then others via empowerment of the Holy Spirit, we are being like Christ and we are fulfilling our destiny as descendants of Abraham. But are we doing this? Do we revere these two profound commandments and live by them with all we are? Let's face the truth of it if we still don't love God with ALL our hearts. All we need to do is assess what we spend the majority of our money and time on. If a significant part of our time is not spent praising God, pursuing God, studying God, portraying God, teaching God, worshiping God, sharing God, representing God, meditating on God, or considering God... If God is not the primary focus of all that we do, the center of it, the motive for it, the purpose in it... then we do NOT love God with all of our hearts. And if that's the case, then something counterfeit, something false, has a hold on us and this gives ample room for the false prophet to reign!

We are told to seek FIRST the Kingdom of God and His righteousness, meanwhile, we water this command down to empty words on a page in the Bible by actually seeking first our OWN hopes, desires, visions, and dreams. Let me say this - even if our dreams are of utmost quality and goodness, if we're chasing them first and not God, we're in a bad place! This is what keeps us from experiencing the promises of the Bible and permits the false prophet to interfere with the plans and purpose of our lives. The fact is, God's promises are true. We WOULD fully experience every promise ever recorded in scripture if we walked in accordance to the reality of the "full message" of the entire scriptural record! And Satan KNOWS this better than WE do! So, I assure you; it is definitely part of the false prophet's operation to keep us from understanding the necessity of embracing our victorious identity in Christ and pursuing righteousness with all our hearts. If we corrected this much in our lives and came to terms with how we ought to sincerely follow ALL of God's commands and stand up boldly in the truth that we are no longer enslaved to sin, this alone would dethrone the false prophet from our lives!

In the early 1900's a very prominent missionary and faith healer of the day, Reverend John G. Lake, delivered many sermons that were recorded and availed to us today. I would like to share some excerpts that I feel most poetically say it all. Reverend Lake begins here by reflecting on his training as a young believer…

> *"In one of these class meetings one day, as I sat listening to the testimonies, I observed that there was a kind of weakening trend. People were saying, "I am having such a hard time." "I am feeling the temptations of the world so much." etc. I was not able at the time to tell people what was the difficulty. I was only a young Christian. But when they got through I observed the old class leader, a gray headed man. He said something like this, "Brethren, the reason we are feeling the temptations so much, the reason there is a lack of sense of victory is because we are too far away from the Son of God. Our souls have descended.*

They are not in the high place where Christ is. Let our souls ascend, and when they ascend into the realm of the Christ, we will have a new note, it will be the note of victory."

Beloved, that is the difficulty with us all. We have come down out of the heavenlies into the natural, and we are trying to live a heavenly life in the natural state, overburdened by the weights and cares of the flesh and life all about us. Bless God, there is deliverance. There is victory. There is a place in God where the flesh no longer becomes a bondage. Where, by the grace of God, every sensuous state of the human nature is brought into subjection to the living God, where Christ reigns in and glorifies the very activities of a man's nature, making him sweet and pure and clean and good and true. Bless His Holy Name.

I call you today, beloved, by the grace of God, to that high life, to that holy walk, to that heavenly atmosphere, to that life in God where the grace and Spirit and power of God permeates your whole being. More, where not only your whole being is in subjection, but it flows from your nature as a holy stream of heavenly life to bless other souls everywhere by the grace of God.

…Beloved, I want to tell you that the soul joined to Christ and who exercises the power of God, ascends into that high consciousness of heavenly dominion as it is in the heart of Jesus Christ today, for He is the overcomer, the only overcomer. But yet, when MY SOUL IS JOINED TO HIS SOUL, when HIS SPIRIT flows like a heavenly stream through my spirit, when my whole

nature is infilled and inspired by the life from God, I too, being joined with Him, become and overcomer, in deed and in truth. Glory be to God." [2]

[2] *Excerpts quoted from pg 50-51 of John G. Lake - His Life, His Sermons, His Boldness of Faith; Published by KCP Kenneth Copeland Publications, Fort Worth Texas ©1994 Kenneth Copeland Publications.*

Things To Consider

Are you trapped in the lie that says because of your sinful nature you are probably never going to change?

Chapter Review Checkpoints

1 Romans 7:18 says, "I know that nothing good lives in me, that is, in my sinful nature. For I have the desire to do what is good, but I cannot carry it out." So, it's hopeless. It's simply not possible to overcome our sin and bad habits.
T or F

2. Romans 6:7, however, says, "We are no longer slaves to sin. For when we died with Christ we were set free from the power of sin." So, this means we are automatically perfect and will never sin again.
T or F

3. But then, Romans 6:11-13 declares, "So you also should consider yourselves to be dead to the power of sin and alive to God through Christ Jesus. Do not let sin control the way you live; do not give in to sinful desires. Do not let any part of your body become an instrument of evil to serve sin. Instead, give yourselves completely to God, for you were dead, but now you have new life." So, this means that we are actually free from the power sin once had over us, but that it is up to us to activate this power within us by choosing to resist sin and instead, choosing to live right.
T or F

4. Finally, Paul shows us in Romans 7: 24-25 NLT, *"Oh, what a miserable person I am! Who will free me from this life that is dominated by sin and death? Thank God! The answer is in Jesus Christ our Lord. So you see how it is: In my mind I really want to obey God's law, but because of my sinful nature (my flesh) I am a slave to sin."* And Romans 8:9 NLT, *"But you are not controlled by your sinful nature. You are controlled by the Spirit if you have the Spirit of God living in you."* So, this means we are still people with a sinful nature which will always try to have its way BUT Jesus Christ has made a way for us to overcome our sinful nature!
T or F

5. The man who says, "I know Him" but does not do what God commands is a _____.

6. 1 John 2:15-16 declares, "Do not love the _____ or anything in the _____. If anyone loves the _____, the love of the Father is not in him. The term missing in these three blank spaces is _____.

7. 2 Peter 1:8 tells us that if we possess certain qualities in increasing measure, then we will stop being ineffective and unproductive in our knowledge of our Lord Jesus Christ. What are these fine qualities that secure our effectiveness?

moral excellence,
and moral excellence with _____,
and knowledge with _____,
and self-control with _____,
and patient endurance with _____,
and godliness with_____,
and brotherly affection with _____ .

8. According to James 4:4-10, God is envious and says our loyalty is divided between God and the world. He says that our friendship with the world makes us _____ of God!

ANSWER KEY - CHAPTER XIII
1-F, 2-F, 3-T, 4-T, 5-Liar, 6-World,
7-knowledge, self-control, patent endurance, godliness, brotherly affection, love for everyone, 8-enemies

Chapter Fourteen
Law vs Grace

If you're saying, "I get it that we are supposed to embrace our in-born victory in Christ. But I just don't understand how there can be a mandate to pursue righteousness if our obedience is not counted unto us as righteousness. If we are saved by grace and not by works... If we are no longer "under the law"... And if it was only counted unto Abraham as righteousness that he "believed" God... How is it that all this hype to obey is not being 'under the law'?"

This is yet another monkey wrench the false prophet utilizes in stifling God's people. He plays games with the believers' understanding of what it means to walk under grace and not the law. The spirit of python sends us all over the place; it merely depends on which tactic would work best on the individual the minion is assigned to. On one end of the spectrum, the mandate for walking in holiness is such that different church organizations lay the burden of regulations on their congregations' shoulders which is a works based faith. On the other end people believe grace is a free pass to continue on in their sin. And then there are those in the middle literally on the fence not knowing if it's scriptural to have to strive to obey God's ways because they think this contradicts the scripture that says we are no longer under the law. The fact is it is somewhat difficult to comprehend what role our obedience does play in the war of law vs. grace.

Consider how even Peter, after everything he had been through with Christ firsthand, after witnessing the Gospel unfold right before his eyes, Peter STILL fell into the snare of assaulting grace by complying with a group of

Jewish 'Christians' who believed the spirit of python that the old covenant law of circumcision remained relevant to their righteousness.

Do we suppose that Peter was confused at what Christ did for him at the cross despite witnessing everything for himself? My opinion is no. I believe he was quite confident that Christ's death fully replaced old covenant regulations which once kept Jews in right standing with God, in as much as they ever could. Galatians 2:12 blames Peter's behavior on the fear of man. My suspicion is that a worker of python assigned to Peter saw this and, because his fear of man was a legal door through which to operate, the devil worker took advantage. Knowing that Peter might buckle at the presence of notable Jewish 'Christians' whom he aspired to be respected by, the false prophet worker played on Peter's fleshly need for acceptance. Without realizing it, Peter's mindlessly shunning being seen with the uncircumcised believers was perverting the gospel to others - which is precisely what the false prophet had planned.

See how the false prophet system works? All these minions are sent out to distort truth and put things into disorder. They'll work through one person's fear and another person's jealousy - whatever works. And all to dismantle truth and promote anything false.

Fortunately, those particular evil sparks never developed into a wildfire but the spirit of python did recognize that the law versus grace conflict was a keeper. Wherever a person was found that he could influence in this way, those same ancient dark workers would spoon-feed gullible believers any distortion that worked. Anything to keep believers from comprehending what it is to walk by grace through faith while still revering the law.

If you have been a believer for any length of time I am confident that, by now, you have heard someone somewhere talking about legalism. We understand legalism to be dirty word, so to speak, because to the contemporary Christian, it's where religion revolves around rules and regulations. It is where grace holds little relevance to one's walk with God and this is distasteful to those of us who embrace that grace is the very heart of the Gospel of Christ! Because we understand that our works are as filthy rags (Isaiah 64:6) and our righteousness is strictly a gift of God through Christ's death for us, we rightfully resist these false prophet induced teachings that push any type of works doctrine.

      This is definitely the right thing, to resist such false doctrines that, for example, cause precious people who love God to think their status with God is contingent upon how many times they pray or how well they do anything for that matter. The Gospel provides it that we no longer have to feel guilty and walk in self-condemnation for our failures. Yet, many organized churches add to the burden of performing instead of promoting the freedom grace offers! They literally add "laws" to our gospel which declares that law and pre-Christ regulations do not make us right with God - which is no longer our gospel! They reduce Jesus Christ to an icon of holiness to emulate and command that when they fail to fulfill this impossible feat, they must go through a series of rituals to be cleansed! It is despicable!

      And then, of course, we have all heard of the phrase "cheap grace" where forgiveness of sins is a free gift and continuing in a life of sin is typical. I don't know too many who blatantly fall for this particular teaching the false prophet promotes but I wonder how many of us do let this wrong interpretation of grace sneak into our thinking on occasion - if ever so subtly?

      Then somewhere in the middle are those of us who are on the right side of grace - who resist both legalism and the opposite extreme that we can go on sinning. But that's not to say the false prophet hasn't messed us over in our understanding of law and grace somewhat as well. I know believers who are under grace who have said, "If you preach at me that I must obey the law then you are trying to put me back under the law!" They feel that any teaching on obedience as a 'mandate' is a law-based doctrine. Not that they desire to be lawless, just that being pushed to strive at obedience might be a legalistic, anti-grace teaching.

I know I wrestled with this for years myself. When I recognized an area of my life where I habitually struggled with a sin, my spirit understood it had to go while another part of me wondered if I was being legalistic. Because if my righteous acts were likened unto filthy rags, and because I am saved by grace through faith in Christ, is my effort to obey minimizing the value of the grace I claim to live by? Did the idea that I "must" obey contradict the very grace I received? I mean, I knew that willfully continuing in sin was not right. But was I trying "to become perfect by my own human effort" the way Galatians 3:3 speaks about? I couldn't make sense of how my purposeful effort to do right was scripturally correct since it was the Old Testament that shouted, "Obey, obey, obey the law!" while the New Testament shouts, "Behold! The law is fulfilled! All you have to do is believe!". There was this unspoken misconception in my circle that born again believers are subject to New Testament teachings, not Old Testament ones which were all about the law.

This was one reason I couldn't find the victory in Christ despite the Bible saying I was a victor in Him. Since I was not yet solid in my understanding of scripture, I wasn't firm in my conviction to always obey. I wasn't resolved to strive for holiness. I listened when the worker of Operation Python whispered seductively into my ear, "Go ahead... It's okay. God understands you are weak in this area. Remember, that's why He gave His life for you, because He knew it was impossible for you to obey all the time. And even when you do right, it's not credited to you as righteous anyway! If you think it's up to you to be righteous, then you are saying you didn't need Jesus to die your death and you are being legalistic and putting yourself back under Old Testament teaching!"

The spirit of python knew exactly how to play me concerning this teaching because he knew I wasn't in the Word deeply enough to get it and he had to keep it that way. And I let him! The attention I gave to the Word of God was always so sporadic. It felt so out of my reach - which I believe was the assignment of yet another Operation Python worker! I can almost hear the commanding officer of the branch, "Keep her AWAY from the WORD no matter what you have to do! Keep her distracted, inundate her with temptations that appeal to her flesh, mess with the soul wounds we inflicted upon her in her youth, exacerbate her depression, overwhelm her, fog up her mind so she can't focus, keep her busy with other things, cause a ruckus with her kids ~ I don't care! Just do everything and anything to keep her out of those scriptures! If we can do that, I don't care how saved she is, she will never be victorious! We'll keep her boggled f-o-r-e-v-e-r!"

The evil commander was right but only to a point. I was so weary, and I was so mentally foggy and emotionally drained with all the setbacks and letdowns in my life that I infrequently delved into the Word of God. I knew it was important and that I should, but it was so out of my mental reach. So I unwittingly allowed the workings of darkness to prevail over me. But what the false prophet didn't count on was that hidden beneath my weariness was the fire of the Holy Spirit and a desperation to overcome. I may have been a fool in how easily it was for him to keep me down all those years, but my drive to find the way out of it was so strong I pursued God harder and harder the more things happened contrary from what I knew scriptures DID say! For example, I knew the Bible said I was supposed to be the head and not the tail, yet, I was the biggest, fattest tail I ever knew! Compared to everyone I knew! Including non-believers!!! No matter how hard I tried or how good I was at something, it didn't work out and I always came out at the bottom! Something was wrong with that picture and I was determined to find out what. This was what finally drove me to fight the fog, to press in past the lethargy, and to go after God and His truths violently! I finally came to a place of desperation for victory and THAT's when the false prophet's tactics against me began to be futile in my life. It was in that pursuit and whole-hearted earnestness for God and His ways that broke me out of the chaotic darkness that lurked in my every corner!

Pursuing the Lord and His truths pays off because I finally came to understand within the depths of my spirit exactly what God does expect from born again believers concerning law and grace.

It's simple. Once you bring the teachings of the whole Bible together, you see that the emphasis on the law in the Old Testament was to establish first, that God is "just" and absolutely disapproves of all sin. Second, to establish what right ways look like compared to wrong ways. And third, the Old Testament serves the purpose of showing that it is impossible to be right with God on our own no matter how hard we try. That the law, which is a righteous, beautiful thing, was actually to our demise since we couldn't perfectly adhere to it. What a fabulous prelude to the Gospel of redemption! Where Jesus Christ would fulfill the law which meant we no longer had to be condemned by our failure to perfectly uphold it! Where, if saved by grace through faith, one is made righteous and old covenant regulation type laws like circumcision and sacrifices or burnt sin offerings were suddenly pointless. Where the burden to obey is no longer dependent upon human abilities but the Spirit and power of God in us! Where we are called to seek the Kingdom of God first and His righteousness (Matthew 6:33). And yes, where we are instructed by Jesus Himself to obey the commandments

(Matthew 19:16-17). Not because they have anything to do with making us right with God, but because walking with God is one in the same with choosing to walk right. Despite it not being what 'makes us righteous'. Not only that, Jesus says in John 14:15 and John 14:21, "If you love me, you will obey my commandments."

For as many times as I heard the story preached about the rich young ruler who asked Jesus, "Good Teacher, what must I do to have eternal life?", I am surprised that the emphasis was primarily on how difficult it was for a rich man to go to Heaven because he doesn't realize his need for God. When I did my own study, something jumped out at me that I never heard reflected upon...

It stuck out to me that Jesus made it a point to ask "Why do you call me good, there is only One who is good." I wondered why He made it a point to do that. Then I proceeded to read His reply to the young man's inquiry on how to acquire eternal life. In the back of my mind was the memory of how Jesus listed the various commandments yet, in the front of my mind I anticipated His answer should have been, "Just believe on Me and you will be saved" or "Repent and believe that I am the way, the truth, and the life..." After all, that is ultimately what we are taught is what it takes to be born of Spirit. But when I saw that my memory had served me correctly and Jesus was, in fact, instructing that the young ruler could have eternal life by obeying the commandments, I was confused. I thought, "But I thought our works can't save us!"

Then it hit me why Jesus said, "Why do you call me good when there is only One who is good?" Jesus was establishing that He recognized that this young man already believed that Jesus was somebody of divine, Holy Authority! In as much as he could at that time prior to Christ's death, the man 'believed' in Christ. So that necessary element was already secured. The next thing

Jesus cleverly showed was that eternal life was, in fact, acquired through obeying His commandments! But I noticed that Jesus only named the six commandments that had to do with loving others but none of the ones that had to do with loving God! And that's when I realized that this was why, after the young man explained he has always followed those six commandments and asked what else he must do, instead of Jesus continuing to list them and naming the two most important ones, "Thou shall have no other gods" or "Thou shall love the Lord your God with all your heart…", he simply exposed the young man's idolatry. He told him to give up that which he idolized and then follow (love and obey) Him above all else.

I always concluded that Jesus wanted believers to remain modest by never being rich because it was never explained 'why' Jesus told the young ruler to give up his riches. The fact is riches were a god to the young ruler. His riches were more important to Him than eternal life! Jesus wasn't saying the only way one could follow Him was to become poor first! He was saying the only way one could follow Him was to have no other gods before Him!

The point is obeying the commandments is a mandate because it demonstrates the decision and commitment to genuinely 'follow' God. Following God means following His ways even though we no longer have to be condemned if we mess up in the process. Because even though following His ways doesn't make us righteous, we are proclaiming our agreement and submission to the only One Who IS righteous Who bestows HIS true, pure, spotless righteousness upon us.

We understand that salvation is what is free and the elements of being born into spirit include believing in Jesus, repenting from sins, and being baptized in water. This establishes how to be saved but doesn't exclude the mandate to follow His ways. So, let's look at this another way…

John 14:6 says, "Jesus told him, "I am the way, the truth, and the life. No one can come to the Father except through me." NLT.

John 1:1 says, *"In the beginning was the Word, and the Word was with God, and the Word was God."* NIV.

1 John 1:1-2 NLT says, *"We proclaim to you the one who existed from the beginning, whom we have heard and seen. We saw him with our own eyes and touched him with our own hands. He is the Word of life. This one who is life itself was revealed to us, and we have seen him. And now we testify and proclaim to you that he is the one who is eternal life. He was with the Father, and then he was revealed to us."*

Let's put this together and see how in one verse Jesus is the way, truth and life, in the next He is the Word, and in the next He is the Word of life! He is additionally named as the one who IS eternal life.

Continuing on...

John 6:62-63, *"Then what will you think if you see the Son of Man ascend to heaven again? The Spirit alone gives eternal life. Human effort accomplishes nothing. And the very words I have spoken to you are spirit and life."* NLT.

Finally, we are shown in Romans 8:4 why God gave us His Son as a sacrifice for our sins. "He did this so that the just requirement of the law would be fully satisfied for us, who no longer follow our sinful nature but instead follow the Spirit." And we are instructed in Galatians 5:16, "So I say, live by the Spirit, and you will not gratify the desires of the sinful nature."

Let's sum up... Jesus first of all is the Word which was the case ever since the beginning of time. And we know the "Word" is scripture wherein the nature, heart, principles, precepts, statutes, and commandments of God are clearly set forth. Therefore, Jesus is saying He "is" the Word, hence, He "is" the commandments, the principles, the ways of God. Meaning the ways of God are God's very essence. Jesus is the summation of the written Word wherein lies ALL the ways and truths of righteousness which are divine life, which includes the totality of the Word (both old and new testaments) which includes BOTH faith in Him AND obedience to the commandments.

Obedience is the demonstration of our faith in Christ! So, if we are instructed to 'live by the Spirit' which is the embodiment of Christ and all His ways, then we are instructed to live righteous lives. For living by the Spirit is NOT living according to the sinful nature but living according to life - which is Christ - which is the Word - which says to obey.

This is why Jesus made it a point to tell the rich young ruler that the way to have eternal life was by obeying the commandments. Not because his righteousness would be established through his works while the rest of the world received grace, but because obeying them "is" walking according to the Spirit which is walking "in" the way, "in" the truth, "in" the life…. in Christ, in GRACE. That passage is the very definition of how one lives who receives eternal life. They love their neighbor as themselves, and they love and obey God above all things.

So, you see, obeying the ways of God (all of them) is one and the same with believing Him. After all, Abraham believed God and THAT is what was credited unto him as righteousness. But just 'how' was it Abraham demonstrated that he 'believed' God? Well, when he….*obeyed* God. This shows that while we are not "under" the law, we certainly should be walking 'in' the law because this is being 'in' Christ Jesus, our Lord.

Things To Consider

It is God's requirement that we do make every effort to walk in obedience through the power of God in us. But not because this is what makes us right with Him, rather, it's what demonstrates that we really are walking with and "in" Him.

Chapter Review Checkpoints

1. The Old Testament is what lays out the laws, commandments, and statutes of God. The New Testament lays out the Gospel of Christ which claims to fulfill the law. Therefore, we are

> A. saved by grace and no longer required to follow the commandments of God.
>
> B. saved by grace only if we commit to following all the commandments of God.
>
> C. saved by grace and made righteous strictly through Christ but still required to show our submission and love for Him by following all the commandments of God.
>
> D. saved by grace so long as we say certain prayers a certain number of times, go to services regularly, celebrate certain feasts, and give away all of our riches.

2. If we think behaving perfectly is counted unto us as righteousness, we are wrong. But we are still required to pursue righteousness by the power of God in us.

T or F

3. We are counted righteous the instant we believe in and receive the shed Blood of Christ Jesus which cleanses us of all sin.

T or F

4. We may no longer have to follow Old Testament regulations such as circumcision and giving burnt offerings as sacrifices, but Old Testament precepts and statutes, such as the Ten Commandments lay out, are the very essence of God's way. Since Jesus is the Way, then, we are certainly required to follow them.

T or F

ANSWER KEY - CHAPTER X1V
1-C, 2-T, 3-T, 4-T

Chapter Fifteen
Withstanding The Resistance

I'm sorry to report that because Satan has a one track mind and sincerely intends to take over the world, His efforts against us will never cease. Certainly, as he loses ground he will be less and less successful at ensnaring us, but the powers and principalities will always be looking for yet another doorway into our lives.

The good news is once we establish our resolve for Christ through our consistency and single-mindedness, the false prophet will realize his efforts against us are more a waste of his time than anything else. But it does take time to establish our unwavering position in the Kingdom of God. Because the devil knows the old programming that we had always lived by and he's resolved to keep us there.

We must understand that in the same way guardian or ministering angels are assigned to us, demonic minions are also assigned to us. And they know us very well. They know what makes us tick. They know what buttons to push - especially since they're the ones who put those buttons into place. They know what strategies work best, when they work best, and how they work best, etc. Not only that, they hear our words and are quick to use them against us if possible. They know our plans and will try to use other people against us if they can as well. They can go to our job interviews ahead of us, for example, and see if they can find a way to influence the outcome. They work continually, looking for any opportunity to hinder us to keep us down, keep us quiet in the Lord, keep us powerless concerning the affairs of God, etc.

This is why we must hide in the shadow of the Almighty! He truly is our strong tower, our refuge and protection from the workers of evil! But only when we HIDE in Him by loving Him, following Him, and standing firm in His truths! When the Risen Lord and His Word truly is our hope and fortress, these minions and powers assigned to us - who will never go away - are kept at bay. Through our hiding in the Shadow of the Almighty and applying His Word to our circumstances, evil is prevented from accomplishing their goals against us! The Lord is so good and faithful and wonderful! When we are 'in' Him, when we are hiding under the shadow of the Almighty, God will reveal the devil's plans against us. He will rebuke the devil on our behalf. He will fight for us and not even let us dash our foot on a stone (Psalm 91:12). He will protect us from disease, disasters, and He says no evil will conquer us! All this if we simply abide in Him and His Word!

Allow me to share something that happened one time...

My husband was having a rough week. He was so tired and sluggish and not really 'there' in our prayer time. He just seemed spaced out. I was praying one night and the Lord spoke to me that the spirit of python was constricting my husband which was why he was so strangely lethargic concerning things. So, we immediately prayed concerning this. The Lord showed where the spirit gained legal access and we repented and closed that door. Suddenly, my husband was lifted and fine again. (See how simple it is to defeat such a mighty worker of darkness!)

That night as we went to bed, I laid down rejoicing and thanking God for revealing what was going on and delivering us from the invisible problem. As I was doing so (my husband was already snoring) I suddenly saw this dark perimeter surrounding us in my mind's eye, like a black force field. Then I saw that to my right, outside of this perimeter, this large dark entity was taking a fit, waving its fists at me violently, cursing at me. This demon was furious at being put out. Suddenly, the evil spirit boldly declared,

"Don't you worry! I WILL get back in! You think you've won??? You KNOW you always fall... You are weak and double minded! You are sure to give me a way. I WILL get back in!"

Immediately, I asked the Lord, "Father, how? How will this spirit of python get back in?" I quieted myself and waited and finally heard the Lord say, "Pride. The spirit will try to get back in through your pride". The Lord also revealed to me the spirit was trying to bring me to fear but God's peace was thick upon me. I was not afraid. The bully failed because I had been 'in' God's presence, will, and heart.

The next day I wrote up scripture versus concerning pride and placed them on the refrigerator to remember the warning so that we would be cautious to not allow pride to rise up in us. Unfortunately, three days later something happened where, believe it or not, my husband and I both very subtly acted in pride towards each other. But the good news is that because the Lord gave us the warning, we CAUGHT ourselves and immediately repented and closed the door! So, the spirit of python was stifled yet again.

And that's all there really is to it - keeping ourselves in line with grace and truth. When we trip we quickly renounce it, thereby rejecting our agreement with darkness, and the door is slammed in the dark worker's face. This is applying and living in the truth.

But let me say this... Be prepared... Especially if you are just now coming out of a lifetime of being under the influence of darkness. If there have been areas and strongholds where the devil has been reigning, you must know that stepping over into the truth and away from their place in your world is always a battle. The dark clouds will not disappear overnight just because you find out what God says and agree with it. You will have to prove your new position over time, through your actions, and even your reactions to what the devil throws at you. You will have to stand the enemy off.

When you first recognize any area where you have been functioning according to the dark kingdom's ways and you begin to bring it under the Blood and walk according to Kingdom of God principles, the attacks will increase for a season. First of all, the spirits who are assigned to you obviously do not want to lose that ground or hold they had on you all these years so the more they inundate you out of their desperation, the more they hope you will grow weary, lose heart, and give up. They know that if you don't stand firm in your new position, and stand to the end, they maintain or regain their hold. They know that sometimes when we decide something, we aren't truly resolved in it because perhaps we are double minded, so they have to break us down and their hope is to discover that it really isn't our resolve after all. Or at least convince us that it isn't. They hope we will conclude that our yielding to truth is pointless because all that ends up happening is things get worse the more we try. They hope to bring us into doubting God in the truth we are trying to apply to our lives. They will do everything and anything to make it look like what we have recently decided to believe about God is a lie and impossible.

More than that, they inundate us because they know we are likely to lose our faith focus if we are surrounded by a slew of problems. They want to overload us with distractions from our primary resolve. If they can preoccupy us with troubles or challenges, weigh us down with disappointments, we will not be as proactive or bold in our faith. What they really want is for us to dwell on those problems because when our eyes are not fixed upon Christ, the enemy gets away with tripping us up all the more. When our eyes are fixed on the problems eventually defeat takes over rather than our hope in Glory and victory in Christ.

Again, just because we recognize the truth and renounce the darkness and our agreement with it does NOT mean the devils will automatically cease and desist. They will continue working the same ways they always had. If it was commonplace for them to interfere with our relationships or make us feel rejected, they'll continue to even though we've removed their legal authority to do so. If it was common for them to devour our finances or curse the works of our hands, they will continue to try even if we begin gving faithfully if they think they can prove to God that we aren't sincere in our resolve. If there is any part of our heart or thinking that is able to yield to the lies or doubt in God's provision again, the devil will find it and bring it out of us! God will certainly rebuke the devourer, but the devourer will keep trying until we prove to him he is wasting his time. Demons are legally able to keep their hold on us unless we truly are resolved in our new position of faith and no longer in agreement with them. So, they won't surrender on the spot. They don't respect the fact that we embraced the truth and are finally attempting to live by it. They could care less. What they'll only respond to is if we really are resolved, remain steadfast, maintain our submission to God's Kingdom, standing firm in our obedience and hope in God - no matter what lies they throw at us, and then finally, ENFORCING the written WORD via the authority of CHRIST against them. Then, and only then, will they finally relent.

But if they push us and taunt us, telling us God's Word will never be effective in our lives, and we back down.... And we grow weary in our well doing... And we grow faint hearted... And we give up trying, believing, obeying... they'll win the battle of rights. And since they know this is always the potential, I assure you, they will go to every length to hold on to the territory they've always monopolized in our lives.

At the end of Christ's 40 day fast, Satan himself tried to tempt Jesus, suggesting he had something to offer the living Christ. He knew he was face to face with the eternal One but he didn't care. He still tried to play Jesus for a fool. Suggesting Christ's identity was inferior to his own. But Christ, knowing Who He was, responded with resolve. There was no wavering. There was no question. Jesus knew Who He was! Yet, it even took Jesus Christ THREE BOLDFACED REFUTES before the devil would back off and leave. Before the devil accepted his defeat and counted it as loss.

How much more will he lie to us, suggesting things are a particular way that they really aren't so that we'll agree with him and take on his ways? So that we'll doubt the Word of God and believe we'll never see the light of day. We have to realize Satan sets out to make sure everything appears to be the opposite as God says it really is.

Renouncing darkness is not the same as putting it out. Putting out the darkness is putting on the ways of Christ and fighting for the truth to the end! We've got to understand, for many demons, we are their personal assignments and have been since we were born. We are their preoccupation. We are their personal missions and obsessions. And their work in our lives is as routine for them is it is familiar and routine for us. So, just because we suddenly see the light doesn't mean they are going to presume we are lost to them! That's when they'll try to convince us otherwise. That's when, more than ever, they'll make our circumstances appear to be contrary to the very truths of God we are trying to lay hold of!

So, again, we must keep our eyes on the Lord. We must not focus on the problems but maintain our resolve for Jesus and His Word. Jesus must always remain at our center! Especially when things get uglier! Realize this is exactly what the spirit of python is trying to control. And then realize that the demons working in our lives aren't going to just walk away upon our new found decisions to live according to Kingdom of God principles. They won't leave until we prove our resolve for God and our faith in Him. And this isn't easy so we should seek much prayer when endeavoring to turn from dark kingdom lifestyles and renouncing our agreements with falsities.

Now what about prayer? We all know we are told to pray without ceasing. But let me confess how, despite knowing this, I have been rather dumb about it over the years.

It hit me like a ton of bricks one day that I had always been in the wrong position that if God spoke something, it was as good as done. As I would discover a truth of God's Word, I'd decide that since I believe it, it would automatically be. After all, God is Sovereign and all powerful. If He said it, that settles it. Period. So be it.

Not so. The Lord finally got this across to me one day. He showed me that His very real and perfect promises are being thwarted and stolen on the constant. He said just because He promises something and releases that certain something doesn't mean a devil isn't going to attempt to keep it from arriving at its destination.

I owe this realization in part to my children. For years, as we experienced relentless setbacks, they would ask why God didn't care about us. My response was always that God did care about us. But then I'd say, "He is going to bless us! When God is ready, He will bless us!

After years of this but only seeing the same, they grew angry and began crying, "You always say that but He never does!"

Much to my dismay, I was training my children to doubt God, His love for us, and His ability to help us. I was not in a right understanding of God and His truths at all. Saying, "God is going to bless us," really showed my ignorance. The Word tells us that His blessings and protection are there for the obedient. The Bible clearly lays it out that God is for His people and when we walk boldly in His righteousness and follow His precepts, then all that He offers is most assuredly availed to us. But you have to know this, for starters, and then you have to stand on it. So when the enemy comes along and interferes with what you have legal rights to according to the Blood of Christ and your submission to it, you tell him to take your hands off of your property by the authority of Jesus Christ given you.

This was what I didn't understand - that my submission to Christ and obedience to His ways meant I was already blessed. The idea that God was 'going' to bless us had no scriptural basis. God already made everything available to those who believed on Him and His work at Calvary... and who walked in the righteousness bestowed on us through the power of the Cross. My poor kids... I was teaching them falsely.

One day in the midst of another struggle when I had said that yet again to my children, the Holy Spirit spoke to me. He said, "Paula, what would you do if you ordered something online or from a catalog and you paid for it upfront on your bank card and, though you were told your package would arrive in two weeks, it never came? Would you say, 'Oh, maybe it'll come next week' and then the following week say, 'Oh, perhaps next week it will surely arrive'?"

I said, "No, certainly not. If my package didn't arrive the very day they said it would, I would call the company or try to track it down using the tracking number." And the Lord replied, "Then why do you not wonder where the packages I purchased for you over 2000 years ago are? Why do you say, 'Oh... they'll arrive.........someday...'?"

The Lord said He purchased my freedom from all bondages at the Cross of Calvary - including setbacks. He said the Cross was his bank card that paid for my freedom in full. And it was shipped all those years ago to arrive in my life upon my redemption. Yet not once have I valued what He bought for me enough to track it or challenge that it may have been stolen or thwarted. He said if the item that I ordered online didn't show up, that perhaps it was because it got put on the wrong flight or the label was misprinted and if I didn't inquire, they may never know to look for the misplaced purchase and ensure its delivery. Likewise, the Lord showed me that if we don't go after what He purchased for us as well, that they could easily become lost to us if we allow it. That we will never receive all He availed to us if we don't look for it, anticipate it, and then take action if we suspect our property has been tampered with. We should be protective and passionate about what He provided for us. I was convicted because I felt the Lord's hurt that we are apathetic concerning the fullness of all He purchased for us that day at Calvary. Did He go through it all in vain? For nothing?

Then He spoke to me about an inheritance. God said that if a person passed away and left a hefty inheritance for me but I never showed up to claim it, until I did, it was not effectually mine. How could I make use of an inheritance that I haven't laid claim to and taken into my possession? Likewise, God's Word avails great things to the believer who obeys the Lord but we must lay claim to these truths as well. They aren't just going to drop into our laps. We must take possession of the truth and make it our own. Especially since there is a devil who is avidly trying to keep us from possessing it.

My goodness, this altered my perspective. I realized that believing truths but then kicking back and putting my feet up presuming these truths will manifest at God's leisure is utter foolishness. No, the Bible says to pray without ceasing and now I understand why. It's because the enemy will gladly thwart every package Father God has destined for us. And then he'll whisper to people like me to not worry about it. To relax because God will come through... someday.

Malarkey. Oh the years I have lost to this demonically twisted perspective. Thank God He is faithful to deliver His children even from false understandings of Him. I truly thought it was up to God to decide when to bless me because He was sovereign. What I grossly failed to realize was His sovereignty provided that I was already blessed since before time began - through His Son! But only if I knew it, believed it, went after it, and took POSSESSION of it.

But just how do we go after things through prayer? In a nutshell, we must pray the Word. But, shall we beg and plead as well? No. Begging God concerning His promises shows you don't believe you already have them - or that He already provided them, rather! This was another lesson I learned. For years I had been pleading with God to send me my husband, my partner in ministry. God was the one who promised him to me, after all. So, I cried and cried out to God to please send him. Finally, a year or so after the Holy Spirit dealt with me concerning my not going after the blessings that were already mine which the devil had thwarted, I was inquiring of the Lord about the husband He promised me. Suddenly, the Lord said, "Paula, why do you ask me for that which I have already provided?"

I wasn't sure what He meant. Then instantly, He brought to my remembrance what He told me about the shipments not arriving. And He said, "I have provided your husband. But the enemy is concealing him from you. Now take authority over that which I have provided for you. Tell him to loose that which legally belongs to you."

I immediately rose up to my feet with fire in my bones. My spirit understood completely. And I went after my package that was shipped to me by God Himself - but thwarted by evil. I said, "Satan, take your hands off my husband! He is mine - appointed to me by the living God Himself! Now loose him, In Jesus' Name!"

My husband found me that very week...

So, what I learned was that I am to earnestly pray for things but to not plead for them. We have to know that everything is already provided and shipped or on its way. We have to be bold in knowing how eager our Father is to bless us, to provide for us that which He promised. How he adores us! And then we have to pray according to what is known. We simply pray the truth!

We are to pray for God's Kingdom to come and His will to be done on earth as it is in Heaven. And we are to stand on His promises, praying them, even out loud, reminding God that He spoke them and that He is not a man that He should lie. Not because He has memory loss, but because we are establishing that we know He said so and we aren't settling for anything but what HE ALREADY SAID. If we know He loves us, and if we know He wants us to be a blessing, and if we know He commands us to be productive and fruitful, and we are doing things His way yet our lives are not manifesting what God says, then we fight for it! We go after it by praying without ceasing for the very truth of God to unfold in our lives. And we don't stop no matter how long it takes!

More than all that, when we pray the truth of the Word and God's promises out loud, we are reminding the devil that we are very conscientious of these truths so he knows he can't get one over on us in the matter. In fact, the more fervent we are in praying the Word and standing on it, the better equipped we are in the truth to not allow the enemy to sneak in.

God made something else very clear to me one day. I was asking Him why it is that if His Word says it and it is in fact, fact, and we believe it, why this isn't enough. Why His promises don't automatically manifest on these premises alone. He is, after all, superior to evil. Evil is powerless against Him. So, how can evil steal our blessings especially when we are in alignment with God's Kingdom and the devil has no legal rights to touch our stuff? And I heard God say, "Because I don't cheat".

The Lord said that He has extraordinary things for us, beyond our imaginations. But He doesn't just dump all of His promises and truths onto us upon our spiritual birth. Salvation is a free gift. Upon redemption, all may enter glory. But He doesn't hand over all the benefits of glory instantaneously. He says no, those who truly want His all and all must go after it with gusto, with fervor... with passion.

What did this have to do with cheating? I wasn't quite sure at first. But, my faithful Lord spelled it out more clearly. He said that if He endowed His wonders on us instantaneously upon coming into the fold of Life, and we all walked in His perfect power, might and blessings automatically, that His power within us to overcome sin would be instantaneous and automatic as well. That our will would no longer be a factor in our overcoming and this, in essence, would be cheating.

God said that it had to be up to us to come into His fullness. It's up to everyone individually to take what they want of the truth and bring it to life in their world. He provided it all, yes! And it is equally availed to ALL who believe. But the benefits are not dropped into our laps on a silver platter without our having a say in it via our devotion, will, and faith in Him. Rather, we will come into as much of His all and all as we personally choose to - according to our own desire and ambition.

Psalm 18:37-40
"I chased my enemies and caught them;
I did not stop until they were conquered.
I struck them down so they could not get up;

they fell beneath my feet.
You have armed me with strength for the battle;
you have subdued my enemies under my feet.
You placed my foot on their necks.
I have destroyed all who hated me."

Note that it says, "I chased... I did not stop... I struck them down..." This shows our role - our responsibility to take action. But then, does it say that because we are super heroes we prevail? Not in the least. It says, "You (Almighty God) have armed me... You (Almighty God) have subdued... You (Almighty God) PLACED MY FOOT on their necks."

It is clear. We have to be proactive and go after the truth regardless of the situation and God then gives us the victory we could never attain on our own.

However, it must be understood that David was accompanied by the hand of God strictly because he had been walking upright with God - according to Kingdom of God precepts and government. It says so in the preceding verses.

Psalm 18:20-26
"The Lord rewarded me for doing right;
he restored me because of my innocence.
For I have kept the ways of the Lord;
I have not turned from my God to follow evil.
I have followed all his regulations;
I have never abandoned his decrees.
I am blameless before God;
I have kept myself from sin.
The Lord rewarded me for doing right.
He has seen my innocence.

To the faithful you show yourself faithful;
to those with integrity you show integrity.
To the pure you show yourself pure..."

You see? God doesn't cheat by empowering us automatically, just because we call ourselves His. It's by our behavior, integrity, and hope in Him we show ourselves His. So, the manifestation of His might and power, then, is up to us!

By earnestly seeking God's Kingdom first and His righteousness and then enforcing the Word by professing it ongoing, by standing on it when the circumstances are lying to us, by persevering to the end in hope and certainty, God's promises come to LIFE in our worlds! And we then SEE the victories we've been reading about for years! By being transformed by the renewing of our minds. By believing God at face value. By applying all His ways and hiding ourselves in His precepts. By believing Him no matter what our circumstances claim and the enemy tries to convince us of! And by praying according to the truth without ceasing - ushering in the very heart, blessings, promises, and will of God for our lives. Praise God.

Things To Consider

Do you know and believe all the wonders God has already availed to you? Do you believe you are, in FACT, already blessed? That His promises are a certainty? Do your prayers reflect this confidence or do they, instead, speak doubt and unbelief?

Are you sluggish and lack ambition and passion to go after the truth? Do you feel too weak to go after the promises of God and make them your reality by fighting the good fight of faith and standing against the liar who is insisting otherwise? Then please pray the following prayer: Father God,

I am Yours and You are MINE! Forgive me, Lord, for all of my sins and lift me. Refresh and renew me now, dear Lord. Deliver me from this snare, from this lack of ambition for You! Give me fight, God! Give me fire! Fill me Holy Spirit! You are the Life in me. You are my hope to overcome and I fall before you now, beckoning Your mighty hand to deliver me! Father, I have been crucified with Christ! It is no longer I that lives, but Christ Who lives IN me! The life I live in this body, I live by faith in the Son of God because He loves me and GAVE Himself for me! (Galatians 2:20.) Shall I squander all You have made available to me? Shall your death be in vain? No, Your death is MY LIFE. And You are IN ME. Now come forth, Light of Life! Rise up in me! Bring LIFE to my dry bones and spur me to battle. I reject every lie of evil I have listened to. I can do this! I can do all things through Christ Who strengthens me! I bind the liar off of my mind, body, soul, and spirit and commit my entire being to YOU, God. For You are a GOOD God and You are faithful to complete what You have begun in me. You will not leave me to this duress. You are my refuge and strength. Now, show Yourself strong, Lord. Show Your strength in me.

Chapter Review Checkpoints

1. Once we make a decision to renounce dark kingdom ways, Satan and all of his evil minions are immediately forced out of our lives and no longer try to hinder us.
T or F

2. If we hide ourselves in Christ, in His truths and ways, God will expose what the devil is up to so that we can overcome
T or F

3. Even though God is with us, when we renounce the kingdom of darkness by coming out of agreement with wrong behaviors, the minions that have always monopolized our lives will not cease and desist. In fact, they will work harder at trying to prove to us that we are wrong about our conviction and faith. They will try to wear us out and even tempt us to just give up.
T or F

4. It is sometimes necessary to seek prayer covering when attempting to come out of a situation where the enemy had control for years and, especially, decades or generations, even!
T or F

5. One way the false prophet worker will try to derail us from our endeavors to overcome and walk in God's ways is by adding new problems and struggles relentlessly. This is all a part of the enemy's strategy and is unavoidable most of the time. So, our part is to

>A. Let the problems and disappointments absorb our focus

>B. Believe the problems are evidence of God's lack of concern for us or power to help us.

>C. Spend all of our time rebuking and casting out the problems

>D. Fix our eyes on Jesus, thank Him that He is with us, praise Him that He is good no matter WHAT garbage the devil dishes out each day, and continue pursuing God's truths and righteousness.

6. We should be protective and passionate about all that Christ provided for us at Calvary. How protective and passionate are you about going after what God provided for you personally on a scale from 1 to 10 - 10 being extremely passionate? Don't be afraid to be honest. Use this as an opportunity to face the truth and come into His all and all.
1 - 2 - 3 - 4 - 5 - 6 - 7 - 8 – 9 - 10

7. If we know God loves us, and if we know He wants us to be a blessing, and if we know He commands us to be productive and fruitful, and we are doing things His way yet our lives are not manifesting the truths of what God says, it's not because God is a liar. It's because the enemy is working to convince us that the Word isn't true. So, we must, therefore

> A. fight for the truth by standing on the Word, declaring it out loud relentlessly
>
> B. pray without ceasing according to what we know and not what we see
>
> C. (if we're walking in alignment with truth) we take authority over that which the enemy is illegally touching.
>
> D. all of the above

8. God doesn't cause His promises to manifest instantaneously upon our redemption. It's up to each believer to possess the truths of God for himself.
T or F

ANSWER KEY - CHAPTER XV
1-F, 2-T, 3-T, 4-T, 5-D, 6-?, 7-D, 8-T

Chapter Sixteen
Forever Abiding

A final key to dethroning the false prophet that I'd like to discuss, which is the very foundation of the Gospel, is understanding and abiding in grace. Yes, a previous chapter discusses the mandate of obeying the law, but now we must drive home the fact that obeying the law should never become what we put our confidence in.

We understand that there are two supernatural kingdoms and that every step we take, every decision we make, is indicative of either one or the other. There is no middle, neutral-ground government. If our behavior is not in accordance to God's truths and policies, then it is of Satan's. Period. And I have attempted to illustrate that by being in agreement (subconsciously or consciously, knowingly or unknowingly) with either God's or Satan's government, the ruling authorities of that government reign.

In order to be sure we're on the 'same page', let's go over the basic truths of the gospel and grace. Because, while the reality is that practicing Satan's ways manifests his authority over us, there's a bit more to what activates the authority of God over us. It's not ONLY our obedience or practicing of God's Kingdom and government ways that subjects us to the benefits of His rule. The key to God's authority manifesting in our lives, BEGINS with our faith in Christ. Again, our obedience to God demonstrates our agreement with God's Kingdom and is why His authority prevails over us. But while our 'works' and 'good behavior' are certainly elemental, we must be sure to realize they are NOT our righteousness. It's rather that we first agree that we are made clean through His Blood, that we are whole and righteous through Him despite our lingering imperfections. Then our love for Him above ourselves and all else which is demonstrated through our obedience to His ways subjects us to the flow of His authority, benefits and power in our lives! It is our agreement that His grace is sufficient, our agreement that His Blood is what qualifies us and then our applying our faith through our submission to Him that subjects us to ALL His power, might, and glory! Period! Even while we are still messed up! Even while Satan's programming still somewhat runs us! It is our AGREEMENT that Jesus is our hope of glory which subjects us to His power and benefits. Our good behavior (or true repentance when we slip) is merely *the evidence that we are in agreement with and truly pursuing Christ.*

I'm just trying to establish that we mustn't walk away from this teaching with a heavy yoke thinking "If I just do better at obeying God, then I'll no longer be subject to kingdom of darkness authority..." This could be dangerous! First, it's not possible to do it on our own, that's why we needed redemption and the power of the Holy Spirit's help in the first place. Second, it's completely untrue. We have to deliberately center everything around what Christ did at the cross and start there. That means we need to walk away from this teaching with faith in our righteousness accomplished at the cross and then live according to the Spirit where we are victorious over sin, thereby demonstrating our agreement to righteousness.

Galatians 5:4 NIV says, *"You who are trying to be justified by the law have been alienated from Christ; you have fallen away from grace."*

If we function under the tiniest of notions that we are justified or reconciled to God by something 'we do' (works), we are not under grace and His benefits are not available to us at all. Because if we rely on the law at all, we are subject to the curse of the whole law which says it's up to us to earn God's provisions and protection - and we can only do so by perfectly obeying Him.

Galatians 3:1-10 NIV says, *"You foolish Galatians! Who has bewitched you? Before your very eyes Jesus Christ was clearly portrayed as crucified. I would like to learn just one thing from you: Did you receive the Spirit by the works of the law, or by believing what you heard? Are you so foolish? After beginning by means of the Spirit, are you now trying to finish by means of the flesh? Have you experienced so much in vain—if it really was in vain? So again I ask, does God give you his Spirit and work miracles among you by the works of the law, or by your believing what you heard? So also Abraham 'believed God, and it was credited to him as righteousness'. Understand, then, that those who have faith are children of Abraham. Scripture foresaw that God would justify the Gentiles by faith, and announced the gospel in advance to Abraham: 'All nations will be blessed through you.' So those who rely on faith are blessed along with Abraham, the man of faith. For all who rely on the works of the law are under a curse, as it is written: 'Cursed is everyone who does not continue to do everything written in the Book of the Law.'* Yikes!

Even though I am striving to reveal the dangerous truth of Satan's power concerning sin and our agreeing with him even unwittingly in breaking God's laws... Even though the reality is that his power is very real and destructive to us when we operate in his ways, the bottom line is not our successful obedience to Kingdom of God principles. The bottom line is realizing and believing that every power, work, and authority of the devil... IS DEFEATED BY THE BLOOD! But only if we are submitted unto it.

Recognizing the truth of devil's power when he gains legal access does not mean we believers now have to sweat and strive to not dare step into his kingdom or we're doomed! No! Fear NOT! Putting our focus on this is not the answer nor is it possible to do on our own! Recognizing the truth that we are subject to Python's ruling authorities when we operate according to his kingdom means we must focus on Christ, repent, love Him with all we are. Then we'll watch Jesus bring us out of the enemy's rule. It's a very beautiful thing.

Please don't perceive the message of this book as 'be good or else'. While it is certainly necessary to come out of agreement with the devil and into obedience to God, it must be understood that we can do it by grace alone. That we qualify for glory because we believe and for no other reason. I repeat: Our obedience merely DEMONSTRATES our FAITH - that we are being reprogrammed by the power of God which is what brings us more and more OUT of agreement with the wrong kingdom, his principles, his standards, his policies, his government, and his ruling authority which has nearly destroyed us. Our works or good deeds are evidence of our FAITH and cement our righteousness, not qualifiers for all of what God offers us. James 2:14-26 NIV explains it this way:

> *"What good is it, my brothers and sisters, if someone claims to have faith but has no deeds? Can such faith save them? Suppose a brother or a sister is without clothes and daily food. If one of you says to them, 'Go in peace; keep warm and well fed,' but does nothing about their physical needs, what good is it? In the same way, faith by itself, if it is not accompanied by action, is dead. But someone will say, 'You have faith; I have deeds.' Show me your faith without deeds, and I will show you my faith by (in) my deeds. You believe that there is one God. Good! Even the demons believe that—and shudder.*

You foolish person, do you want evidence that faith without deeds is useless? Was not our father Abraham considered righteous for what he did when he offered his son Isaac on the altar? You see that his faith and his actions were working together, and his faith was made complete by what he did. And the scripture was fulfilled that says, "Abraham believed God, and it was credited to him as righteousness," and he was called God's friend. You see that a person is considered righteous by what they do and not by faith alone. In the same way, was not even Rahab the prostitute considered righteous for what she did when she gave lodging to the spies and sent them off in a different direction? As the body without the spirit is dead, so faith without deeds is dead."

Roman's 8:10-14 NIV says, "But if Christ is in you, your body is dead because of sin, yet your spirit is alive because of righteousness. And if the Spirit of him who raised Jesus from the dead is living in you, he who raised Christ from the dead will also give life to your mortal bodies through his Spirit, who lives in you.

Therefore, brothers, we have an obligation—but it is not to the sinful nature, to live according to it. For if you live according to the sinful nature, you will die; but if by the Spirit you put to death the misdeeds of the body, you will live, because those who are led by the Spirit of God are sons of God."

We already understand... because of the fall of man in the Garden of Eden we have all been born 'dead'. That's what this is saying. Not just spiritually dead, either. But our physical bodies, according to Romans 8:10, are dead because of sin. Yes, we are walking around and breathing, but dead in that our bodies are subject to death and destruction unlike the divine bodies we will have in Heaven which I believe Adam and Eve HAD before the fall.

But the good news is that if by the Spirit (who lives in us - Who raised Christ's PHYSICAL body from the dead) we put to death the misdeeds of the body (sin), we will LIVE! Romans 7:6 NIV says, *"But now, by dying to what once bound us, we have been released from the law so that we serve in the new way of the Spirit, and not in the old way of the written code."* Hence, our good works is our submitting to and obeying the Holy Spirit in us who compels us according to the ways of God. And even though the ways of the Spirit are the same as the nature of the written law - because they both came from God and 'are' God as we previously discussed - it is only to our benefit to submit to the Spirit by faith since relying on our submission to the written law leaves us dead in our lack of obedience to the whole law. Whereas the heart that lives in submission to the Spirit through faith (even if our sin nature creeps in from time to time) has LIFE. This means the life the Spirit gives our mortal bodies is restoration, healing, wholeness, wellbeing, and vitality!

There is no reason to fear the reality of the kingdom of darkness and it's ruling forces that we have unwittingly permitted to reign over us any longer. Because while the power we have granted Satan in our un-knowing is real and often times, devastating, by our now knowing the power of the Blood and who we are in Christ, we can start each day in confidence that the victory is ours regardless of what remnants of our previous, dead selves remain! We can relax and trust that in our pursuit of God, He'll expose where the devil has a hold in our lives and help us to bring him under Christ's authority. But to not fear it; to not be overwhelmed in seeing where we still fall short thinking we're, therefore, under the false prophet's power and never going to see victory. Because when we recognize an area that is not right or if we are experiencing demonic interference in our lives, all we simply need to do is take it to the cross and Python's power is instantly nullified. We simply ask God to address or expose whatever it is we need to know as to why the enemy is getting away with stuff. We repent and seek forgiveness if the Holy Spirit convicts us about something and the result automatically is that Satan's hold becomes null. And in seeking God, He will reprogram us more and more according to Holy Kingdom principles and override Satan's along the way.

Unfortunately, however, so long as we resist the truths God is trying to convey, or simply neglect our relationship with God and the transforming power of His Word, so long as we fail to seek His Kingdom First and His Righteousness... the longer we will remain subject to some measure of dark authority. These are the primary reasons we believers go in circles. We fail to realize the necessity of consuming God's Word and Truths and seeking His Kingdom and righteousness first with all our hearts. We fell for the trap of thinking our kind Christian hearts and going to church every week were enough.

It bears repeating: Knowing the power and truth of the Blood of Christ shed at the cross is the key to coming out of python's grip. Satan is POWERLESS against one who truly knows Christ intimately!

Again, not a single chapter in this book has been dedicated to teaching on the casting out of demons. There certainly is a time and place for it, but I gave it the measure of emphasis required. That's because I believe the Lord wants to emphasize the importance of knowing who we are, who HE is in us. He wants us to let Him truly be our Lord and all in all because that's where Satan is powerless. Sure, the Holy Spirit will quicken us to command a spirit to go or cast out demons, yes... But we don't start there. We start by getting right with God because if we are pursuing God and His righteousness with all our hearts, He will guide us to do what we need to in a given moment. We don't have to study 'how to stomp out the devil', we have to study God.

The bottom line is grace. Dethroning the false prophet is completely possible through determining to saturate ourselves with the truth of the Gospel! Like I said, it took me over twenty years to come out of Python's many grips. Oh, I sincerely chose God and practiced His obvious truths, but I did not consume Him. He wasn't my first priority and lover. My 'self' desperately got in between me and God. I was double-minded so I easily fell for Python's strategies. I believed the lies that I was weak and would never get anywhere in this life. I hated myself and was easily wounded because of past hurts. These ways were dark government ways! And they empowered the empire to suffocate me! I didn't understand the love of God nor the power within me to overcome sin. I could go on and on! Putting it frankly, I had one foot in the Kingdom of Heaven, and one foot in the kingdom of darkness. But had I pressed in to the shadow of the Almighty harder, had I saturated myself in the Word of God, connected myself to mighty people of God who could cover me in prayer and hold me accountable... Oh, how much sooner I would have known this freedom!

APPLYING WHAT WE KNOW

First, and assuming you already are, we must be saved through faith in Jesus Christ. But we are to understand that the truth of the Gospel means it is by grace we have been saved through faith, not by works. And also, that we do not cheapen the grace of God by continuing in acts we know scriptures declare to be wrong. We must realize that our faith in Christ demonstrated by our walking in obedience to His ways and truths are counted to us as righteousness. That this is what brings LIFE to both our eternal and the current physical condition of our previously sin-cursed, mortal beings. And last, understand the breadth of what the salvation of Christ is for us - which, when we abide in Him, is not only reconciliation to the Father and eternal life but also abundant life here on earth.

This means wholeness, full health and wellbeing, prosperity, power, and miracles are ours according to our faith and submission to Christ Jesus our Lord.

In other words, if you want to be victorious over the false prophet, simply BELIEVE that God said you already are. Your knowing is to his demise.

Once we are saved we must search God's heart as to what HE says about us. We must pursue Him and His ways with all that we are. Saturate yourself in the Word of God which transforms us! Praise Him constantly. Choose joy even if and when you are in the middle of a storm and all seems unfair or unjust. Speak that which is lovely and good. Do not profess or talk about any of the ugliness that is all around you - don't feed it the energy it craves to remain in existence! The devil wants us talking about our problems because that empowers them to remain! So, only speak and meditate on that which is good. Study God through His written Word, listen to scripture through worship music in place of secular. Not because all secular music is tainted (though most is) but because LIFE is in the WORD and Christian music contains the Word. Work out your salvation with fear and trembling. Seek out teaching after teaching through television, books, the internet, or recordings. The more you saturate yourself... surround yourself with the Word of God, the more you are being regenerated by the Author of Life. The more the Light of Life becomes your very essence. It is power. It is transforming.

Also, give thanks continually and fix your eyes on Jesus. If there's anything noisy in your flesh which demands you to pay more attention to it than God, crucify it! Shut its mouth! Cut it off! You may need to fast to show your body it isn't Lord over you. The Bible tells us to fast anyway. Keeping our flesh at bay is one reason why. You can fast from favorite foods for a season, or complete meals for shorter periods. You can do partial fasts long-term or complete fasts short-term. You can even fast from favorite activities or hobbies. Anything to say, "Hey, I give this up to my Lord in declaration that He is Who is more! God reigns over me in every way!"

Pray in your coming in and going out! And ponder continuously how much mercy, grace, goodness, and unmerited favor the Mighty Living God has for you ALWAYS! Humbly but passionately pursue your God, believe Him, hold fast to Him, and let Him guide you into your freedom. Pursue His Kingdom and His Righteousness and His Will (not yours) and you'll start seeing the spirits which have operated against you all of your life fall away in miserable defeat!!!

Yes, pursue God with your whole heart! Do all that He asks and guides you into. Don't hold back and don't be casual about your relationship. Get to know Him for real! His love for you is greater than any other love! Walk in love always, not selfishness. Give generously and cheerfully taking communion as often as you wish in remembrance of Him.

Concerning communion, realize you don't have to clean up before taking it. 1 Corinthians 11:29 KJV says, "For he that eateth and drinketh unworthily, eateth and drinketh damnation to himself, not discerning the Lord's body." Discerning the Lord's body? Since discerning means showing insight and understanding, this means a person who takes of the bread and cup without their heart observing Christ's death is in trouble. We are to partake of the Lord's Supper to honor Christ and proclaim our Lord's death until He comes. Taking it because we're hungry or want to fit in with the crowd at church if we could care less about what Christ did is dangerous! That's why we're instructed to examine ourselves to ensure our partaking is for remembering His sacrifice.

I believe this is misconstrued as meaning we can't take communion if we are in a bad way. And we think we have to be victorious over that issue before we qualify to receive communion. Yes, I do believe that if we are truly honoring Christ's death and resurrection that in our coming to partake of the Lord's Supper we will humble ourselves and confess if we've been in disobedience to Him. But it's more so that we come to Him saying we know we are wretched apart from the righteousness His death brought us. And we partake declaring we honor His gift to us! For as often as we do it, we do it in remembrance of Him!

Finally, dethroning Python means not agreeing with him anymore. So as the Holy Spirit brings things to your attention, deal with them. Surrender, confess, submit… No matter how much you feel addicted to it, accustomed to it being a part of you, profess with your mouth that you reject it; renounce it. And continue to do so even if you don't feel it in your bones yet. Your bones will catch up eventually. Just stand on the truth, speaking the Word of God concerning the issue that isn't right within you. Command it to go and your flesh to come into compliance with truth. Again, fast if you must. Just show the issue who is Lord. Show it you are in agreement with the Mighty God and resist your affiliation with darkness. Replace the false action/behavior with a Godly one. Because HE is your pursuit!

And guard your MIND in Christ Jesus! Remember, that's how the false prophet gets to us most! Through our thoughts. So, be alert to your own thinking patterns and processes. Take them all captive and bring them all into the obedience of Christ. If there's anything negative, unlovely, impure, unholy.... Get rid of it!

Whatever you do, do NOT allow the enemy to isolate you no matter how badly you crave it! Don't feel sorry for yourself – it's a trap!

Seriously, don't believe any of his lies any longer! You are an heir to the throne. The enemy is YOUR footstool. He has simply tricked you into thinking that YOU are the footstool. But you are NOT. And don't believe those thoughts that nobody likes or loves you, nobody cares, life's too hard, etc. Poppycock! He's a liar! Find the truth in the Word and declare it aloud!

We must be vigilant and on purpose! GET THIS! And I'm speaking this to myself, as well! Operation Python is about twisting the entire Body of Christ up so badly and keeping us believers from recognizing and coming into the WHOLENESS which is provided for us.... And he will stop at nothing to accomplish this to whatever degree he can! These spirits are assigned to keep us as far from God and full truth as possible and they will work tirelessly to accomplish it. And why? Because we become POWERFUL when we finally grasp it.

So, know WHO YOU ARE and how it is that Python's authority is entirely subject to YOU! To YOUR agreement and acceptance of any aspect of his government and policies. But also and more importantly, come into agreement with the FULL truth of the power of the Blood of Christ, pursue God with all you are, and watch as you come more and more OUT of agreement with the ways of darkness.... Which is your CERTAIN and ABSOLUTE DESTINY!!

Ephesians 2:1-5 (NIV)

"As for you, you were dead in your transgressions and sins,
in which you used to live when you followed the ways of this world and the ways of the ruler of the kingdom of the air, the spirit who is now at work in those who are disobedient. All of us also lived among them at one time, gratifying the cravings of our sinful nature and following its desires and thoughts. Like the rest, we were by nature objects of wrath. But because of his great love for us, God, who is rich in mercy, made us alive with Christ even when we were dead in transgressions—it is by grace you have been saved."

Chapter Review Checkpoints

1. We must obey God's commandments but be very careful not to feel our doing so means we 'earned' all of God's promises and blessings.

                      T or F

2. While it is up to each person to determine to go after the fullness of God by saturating themselves in His Word, seeking Him with all they are, and obeying His ways, it is strictly by grace that we can do it at all. The truth is we have been pardoned from what we deserve but now, may freely come into the all and all of Christ.

                      T or F

3. If we work really hard at obeying God's ways and casting out the devil, we will surely prevail against the false prophet.
T or F

4. The bottom line to attaining victory in Christ is realizing and believing that every power, work, and authority of the devil is defeated by the Blood of Christ.
T or F

5. James 2:14 says, "What good is it, my brothers and sisters, if someone claims to have faith but has no deeds?" This means

    A. they say they are Christians but don't demonstrate it in their actions or behavior

    B. they say they are saved but don't care to obey

    C. they say they believe but don't pursue righteousness

    D. all of the above

6. Abraham was considered righteous because he _____.

7. But the way Abraham demonstrated his belief was by obeying whatever God told him.
T or F

8. According to Romans 8:10, If Christ is in us, our bodies are dead because of sin but are alive because of righteousness. This means that if we live BY THE SPIRIT then that same Spirit which raised Christ from the dead will bring divine LIFE to our mortal bodies!
T or F

9. If we come into the full LIFE of Christ that is already birthed in us, then the false prophet is powerless against us.
T or F

10. The key to completely dethroning the false prophet from our lives is to completely abide in Christ.
T or F

ANSWER KEY - CHAPTER XVI
1-T, 2-T, 3-F, 4-T, 5-D, 6-Believed, 7-T, 8-T, 9-T, 10-T

Final Prayer

Dear Heavenly Father,

Thank You, Father, that You are for me and that there is no power greater than Yours! Oh, God, You are sovereign and put everything into place. I understand that the prince of the air has legal rights because of our sin but Father, You made a way through Your Son that we could overcome and now I plead the Blood of Jesus Christ over every area of my being, inside and out, where I have allowed the enemy access! Father, I have been naïve and foolish! I want to love You first – I want to lay down my affair with the world and all the things that compete for my favor. Father, please forgive me. Please cleanse me of every false thing in me! Help me to lay down my life, my self, all my false idols, everything that stands between us. Father, I know I must be ONE with You in every sense of the word. But I cannot do it without Your help. What I have known (strongholds, ideals, passions, perspectives) have been such a profound part of who I am and they run deep. These are to my demise but Father, I don't know how to let go of them! Please, You are the power, the One Who transforms. PLEASE transform me miraculously right now. Please deliver me from all evil and every false thing in me right now. Oh God, I cry out for Your mercy to help me in this. It is my will to love You first, but the programming of my flesh is grotesquely against You! Father, I repent of this. I do not want to be this way. You are my only hope in overcoming.

Okay, You say I can do all things through Christ Who strengthens me, then so be it. I can love You with all my heart, mind, soul, and strength – through Christ Who strengthens me! Glory to You, my King!

And Father, I declare that I will come into every plan and purpose YOU have destined for me. I lay hold of it all right now. I renounce every lie I have ever believed. I repent of every doubt I ever had in You, Precious Lord, the only One Who is truly FOR me! I believe You love me and I declare I will now comprehend this love, this profound love, like NEVER before. And I will blossom in the inheritance You provided me at the cross – and all of its fullness therein. I declare I shall obey You, I take up my cross and follow You, I lay down my 'self' and turn my eyes and ears to You only. Bless You, Mighty God. For nothing compares to You. And You will finish the work You started in me. You have specific plans for me and I yield to it all right now. Father, help me to see everything I have going on in my life that is vain and useless. Help me to identify all which needs to go. You are so good to me, my Lord!

Father, You say You have gifts for each of us to walk by the Spirit of God that we may do greater works than Jesus did on earth. Please grant unto me the manifest power of Your Holy Spirit that I may overcome and walk in the very power Python does not want me to know. Lord, restore unto me all the years lost because of Python's infiltration in my life. Yes, I know it was my ignorance that he got away with it, but I repent and bring it all under Your Blood whereby all is made new. This is my fresh start in You, Father. Now rectify all that Python has destroyed and hindered in my life. Restore all that was meant to be, even that which I knew nothing about. I align myself with You, Father, and while I have so much yet to learn, I know it is all about Your power and Spirit that anything is accomplished. So, in Your mercy, put me on the path upwards. Remove every work Python has in place, every assignment, every plot. I ask that You bring me into Your authority to where the enemy knows I am One with You and that he can no longer get away with his tactics.

Thank You, Father, that I am free because of You. You have rescued me from the dominion of darkness and transferred me into the Kingdom of Your dear Son! (Colossians 1:13).

You go before me, Lord, and follow behind me. Please help me to abide in You always. Do not let me go astray. Do not let me fall for Python's strategies to lure me back into old programming. God, have mercy and keep me close to You. I confess I am weak but You are strong in me. Please hear this prayer and set my feet on the solid rock of hope, Christ Jesus. He is my refuge and strength. Where would I be without Him. So, please keep me. Open my eyes and ears to hear EVERY word You would say to me. Download spiritual truths and insights unto me, as I am desperate for You to take over. Oh, God, help me to pray without ceasing. Take over me, Holy Spirit. Rule me. And let me come into the power of God for Your sake, Father. Let me rise up and become the very thing Python has been trying to prevent ALL MY LIFE!!! Let me do double damage to the dark kingdom for all his efforts have cost me. You are the righteous One, God, and I declare I will know You most intimately, I will love You with all I am, and I will be all You have called me to be. In Jesus' Name, Amen.

My Heart's Desire Evaluation

For real now...
Who holds first place in your heart?

We can find this out by assessing where our passions lie.

The Bible tells us that if we seek God, we will find Him when (and only when) we seek Him with ALL our hearts. It additionally tells us to love God above all things. And it tells us to seek first the Kingdom of God and His righteousness so that all of our other desires will be added unto us. The following is an evaluation tool that will give us perspective on this. While it cannot be perfectly conclusive, I'm confident that it will in the very least help us to recognize how our priorities and instinctual interests reflect if God really is first in our hearts. This, then, correlates with how easy it may be for demonic forces to influence our lives. Because for the measure of our hearts' drive is for anything other than God is the same measure the devil can invade.

There are two parts to the evaluation. You will go through each part giving a score value to each question [0 to 4]. After completing the evaluation, you will be instructed on how to determine your final score.

Please understand, this evaluation was not created to establish how mature or perfect we are as Christians. Jesus said if we love Him we will obey Him. But this evaluation is directed more towards identifying where our focus and interests lie. Because the more we love Him, the more our interests, activities, and focus naturally revolve around God. The evaluation really has nothing to do with sin level or victory over sin or anything like that. It's strictly a tool to assess our interest levels.

Please do not stress over this Keep in mind that we were born putting ourselves first. We've lived all our lives learning how to consider others before ourselves. Then we receive Christ as our Savior and we find out He wants us to lay ourselves down completely, to live completely selfless lives, to seek after His heart first, His ways, His

Kingdom, and His righteousness ABOVE EVERYTHING! It's not easy, especially in this day and age where self is ridiculously exulted like never before in history. So, relax and be as honest with scoring yourself as possible - but not overly critical either! Write your scores on a separate sheet of paper to keep it private if you must, just be sure to be truthful.

Please note... If you feel shame or self-condemnation while answering the questions honestly, that is the enemy and you need to command him to shut his mouth in the name of Jesus! Self-condemnation and fear are anti-scriptural - they are of dark kingdom government. These are Satan's policies, not the Lord Jesus Christ's. So if you allow such thoughts or feelings then you are agreeing with policies of hell. Take such thoughts captive and bring them into the obedience of Christ. Do not give the evil spirit, who is under orders right this minute by Python to shut you down, legal access to your life! God is for you and He already knows the condition of your heart better than you ever will so don't worry about anything! Don't be afraid to see yourself as you really are. If you are a perfectionist and fear facing where you may fall short via the evaluation, let go of that, too! You aren't supposed to be perfect because you wouldn't need God if you were!

You will begin with Part A by reading each item and deciding how strongly it applies in your life. If it's something that absolutely never applies to you, you give it a 0. If it's something that is tremendously true to the extreme, something you are passionate about or obsessive over, you give it a 4. If it is something that is true once in a while or occasionally applies, then 2. And of course, you give it a 3 if it more than occasionally applies but isn't something over the top. And you give it a 1 if does apply, but very seldom. ~Feel free to use point fives (halves) as well. I found that I had to do this quite frequently when taking the evaluation myself.

I want to explain before you take the evaluation that your final score will be anywhere from -4 to 4. Obviously, the closer you are to 4 will show that your interests and focuses are more on God than self. Likewise, the closer you are to -4, the more your interests and passions are anything but God. Again, it's not an indication of how obedient or sinful you are. It strictly measures the heart's interests. And it is my contention that nobody on earth can score a perfect 4. But... could I be wrong?

Let me also say ahead of time that if you end up scoring a 0, don't be alarmed because this means that at least HALF of your heart is resolved for Christ! So that's a good thing. It may or may not mean you're in danger of being "lukewarm", however, so I encourage you to really take a look at why it is you score as you do. Let God show you some things He wants to.

Last, understand that falling in love with God and His being first in our heart in every way truly is a process that happens only as we go after it and say "no" more often to self or the things of this world. Remember, our instinct or nature is for self so a person that loves God first really had to sow towards that. They literally had to choose to lay themselves down just as we need to do. They weren't born in love with God. Everyone has to decide to go after God more and let Him capture us, woo us, and sweep us off of our feet. I pray this evaluation will help you do just that.

"My Heart's Desire Evaluation"

Use the following Score Chart to help to determine how DETERMINED or COMPELLED you are concerning each item. Use .5s where applicable:

    0 NEVER, NOT A CHANCE

    1 SELDOM, BARELY, MINIMAL INTEREST, ONCE IN A BLUE MOON

    2 SOMETIMES, YES BUT FAR & FEW BETWEEN, CONSISTENTLY BUT BRIEFLY, RELATIVE INTEREST, CAPTIVATED ON OCCASION

3 QUITE A BIT, PRETTY OFTEN, STRONG INTEREST, FAIRLY DRIVEN, FREQUENTLY CAPTIVATED

4 ALWAYS, EXTREMELY DRIVEN, OBSESSIVE IN THIS, CONSTANT INTEREST, CONSUMED WITH

EVALUATION - **PART A**

1. You spend a lot of time listening to Christian ministry or teachings outside of church or Bible studies such as Christian television, tapes/CDs/books; browsing or researching topical studies indicative of scripture truths; researching scripture; doing in depth studying to understand certain teaching, perhaps find out what the original Greek or Hebrew texts say and comparing with current versions -

2. You give generously and you routinely give significant alms (monies that help the orphans or poor, for example) even if your income isn't extraordinary -

3. You think about how much you want to be a blessing to others, to God, to the world. You wish you had more money to give to orphans or to do things like help dig water wells. You think about growing as a believer so that you can make more and more of a difference in this world for the Kingdom of God -

4. You often talk about what God is showing you, what He spoke to you, what you think He wants you to work on, where you think He is taking you, what He wants from you -

5. You admire people of God who go to the ends of the earth serving and promoting the Kingdom of God - teaching, ministering, and

changing lives. Such as Billy Graham and missionaries and others who truly go above and beyond the call -

6. You consistently spend a great deal of time reading and meditating on the Bible; praying, worshiping -

7. If you have extra money you had not expected, and all of your financial obligations are met, you typically try to give at least some of it if not all of it to a favorite ministry or charity in addition to all that you already give -

8. You spend a great deal of time thinking about God - always considering God, wishing to see, hear, or touch Him. Wishing you could just climb a ladder to heaven and visit Him in any given moment that you please –

9. Whether you can afford it or not, when a sincere need is presented to you, you deeply desire to help -

10. You talk about how awesome God is, how He's done so much for you, how you are so thankful that He saved you and spared you. You talk about where you once were compared to now. You talk about not being able to imagine your life and where you would be had God not intervened when He did. You talk about how much freedom and blessing you have found in Christ even if there are still troublesome areas in your life -

11. You admire people who have the light of God shining brightly within them - who are always touching people one way or another with the Love of God

12. You are frequently volunteering for a cause or giving of your talents & skills for the benefit of somebody's well being or the Kingdom of God, or working on spiritually related projects (like for church, Bible study, reading or writing a Christian book) -

13. You frequently well up with thanksgiving and hum or sing praises to God or listen to your own worship music outside of services, perhaps while doing chores or driving. You find yourself thanking God throughout the day. You quickly choose to delight in God even on yucky days -

14. You talk about your ideas for ministry or helping on a committee or in your neighborhood or something where you want to find a way to make a Godly difference for the better. You talk about and find ways to be a blessing one way or another, big or small

15. You admire and actively support political entities who promote Kingdom of God principles -

TOTAL PART A = _____

Next you will take Part B of the evaluation. Please realize that the questions in part B are not all "bad". Most are pretty much natural aspects of living that are even to our health and benefit. Remember that it's only when these other things monopolize our hearts that they are bad. So, in order to accurately assess your heart, be sure to answer each item truthfully. Just as you did in Part A, choose the score value that demonstrates how strongly the item applies to you -

EVALUATION - **PART B**

16. You spend a lot of your free time enjoying hobbies or other interests (i.e. painting, sports, musical instruments, politics, sailing, mountain climbing) or working on NON spiritually related projects (around the house, homework for school, catching the news, writing a book) -

17. You frequently talk about yourself, your dreams for retirement, your plans for vacation, your longing for a fancy car or boat or other material items -

18. You typically try to make sure to reward yourself with something (material item, a getaway, break, etc.) that's just for you at least once a month. Especially if you routinely do for others -

19. You frequently listen to secular music in the car, on your MP3, or around the house -

20. You love to go on frivolous shopping sprees (mall, catalog, or internet) pretty frequently. Especially if you have a "collection" to maintain or you are compelled to keep up with the Jones' or always stay in style by acquiring the latest trends -

21. You frequently think about the things you desire like your soul mate, the vacation you never had or even your next vacation or trip around the globe, having a child, your dream home, your dream career, or whatever else that you think will be the answer to your dreams –

22. Relationally, you frequently spend your time chatting (NON spiritually) with friends (in person, phone, texting, Facebook - playing with kids - romance/intimacy with spouse outside of bedtime) -

23. If you have extra money you had not expected, and all of your financial obligations are NOT met, you are still likely to purchase that certain something you'd been wanting for awhile. You may even charge it -

24. You admire people who are highly educated or those who have profound careers and success –

25. You frequently spend your free time lounging, watching non-Christian television/movies, snacking, reading non-Christian materials or playing games (any type; cards, video, internet), browsing internet, leisure shopping -

26. You dwell a lot on your own or other people's problems and difficulties of life, wondering why things never get any better. Wondering if or when the blessings will ever start coming -

27. You continually talk about all the things going wrong in your life that you aren't happy about - like what went wrong at work, how the kids are still misbehaving and acting out, how the in-laws are still causing flack, how the neighbors are still being pesky, etc. -

28. You admire people who have everything they could ever desire - from cars to their annual, extravagant, luxury vacations. You envy people who spend their retirement leisurely enjoying life to the full and hope you will be so fortunate to do likewise -

29. You talk about how nothing ever goes right in your life while everyone else seems to be a blessing magnet. You express that you feel you'll never get your break or the blessings you deserve -

30. You admire famous musicians, actors, or other celebrities because 'they've got it made' or they've got everything going for them - I.e. looks, health, charisma, money, fame –

TOTAL PART B = _____
Now take Total A minus Total B.

Next take your new total and divide by 15.
The result will range between -4 and +4.
Remember, a 0 means 50% of your heart puts God first!

A ____ minus B ____ = ____ / 15 = ____

Printed in Great Britain
by Amazon